HUNDRED PERCENTERS

CHALLENGE YOUR EMPLOYEES TO GIVE IT THEIR ALL AND THEY'LL GIVE YOU EVEN MORE

MARK MURPHY

SECOND EDITION

Mc Graw Hill Education

New York   Chicago   San Francisco   Athens   London   Madrid
Mexico City   Milan   New Delhi   Singapore   Sydney   Toronto

1 2 3 4 5 6 7 8 9 0   QFR/QFR   1 9 8 7 6 5 4 3

ISBN   978-0-07-182556-6
MHID 0-07-182556-8

e-ISBN   978-0-07-182560-3
e-MHID 0-07-182560-6

Library of Congress Cataloging-in-Publication Data
Murphy, Mark A. (Mark Andrew)
   Hundred percenters : challenge your employees to give it their all, and they'll give you even more / Mark Murphy. — Second edition.
      pages cm
   ISBN 978-0-07-182556-6 (alk. paper) — ISBN 0-07-182556-8 (alk. paper) 1. Employee motivation. 2. Achievement motivation. 3. Goal setting in personnel management. 4. Supervision of employees. I. Title.
   HF5549.5.M63M867 2014
   658.3'14—dc23
                                                       2013028484

McGraw-Hill Education books are available at special quantity discounts to use as premiums and sales promotions or for use in corporate training programs. To contact a representative, please visit the Contact Us pages at www.mhprofessional.com.

To Andrea, Isabella, and Andrew

Contents

Acknowledgments

I hate to be cliché, but there really are too many people to thank individually for making contributions to this book. My team of several dozen researchers and trainers and each of our hundreds of fantastic clients deserve a special thank you. This book and the research behind it wouldn't exist without all their efforts.

I would like to highlight three individuals who made special contributions to this particular book.

Andrea Burgio-Murphy, PhD, is a world-class clinical psychologist, my wife and partner through life, and my creative sounding board. Since we started dating in high school, I have learned something from her every single day. My personal and professional evolution owes everything to her.

For numerous reasons, including the continued growth at Leadership IQ, this book seemed to take me away from home more than previous books. My children, Isabella and Andrew, deserve a special thank you for continually reminding me of what's really important.

While everyone at Leadership IQ is important, the following folks deserve a special thank you for their close work with me and their extra effort to help make this book possible. In alphabetical order, they are: Lyn Adler, an exceptional writer who has worked with me for several years and whose assistance made it possible to distill mountains of research and interviews into this contribution to the leadership literature. Cheryl Arnold ensures that the attendees of the webinars I personally deliver receive world-class support and service. Lauryn Franzoni, our president, ensures that our market strategy attracts the right kinds of organizations to further build our community of Hundred Percenter clients. Corey Laderberg and Meaghan Joynt are our two top business development specialists, and because they work so closely with me, they have taken on special responsibilities to ensure that we continue to work with exceptional organizations. John Sheehan is our data guru and chief software architect, and he translates big data into absolutely brilliant insights. Jeffrey Sherman directs our client operations and enables all of us to deliver so much value to so many organizations.

Mary Glenn, associate publisher at McGraw-Hill, deserves a very special thank you for recognizing the need for this book and making the process fast and smooth. After working with Mary and the team at McGraw-Hill, it's very clear to me why the best business thinkers sign with them.

For More Information

For free downloadable resources including the latest research, discussion guides, and forms, please visit www.leadershipiq.com.

Introduction

Here's a question for you: What percentage of your employees feel inspired to give their best effort at work?

I'm not asking if your employees do a decent job, or if they work well together, or even if they seem reasonably satisfied at work. No doubt you've got a nice group of people who do good work, get along with you and one another, and are generally well intentioned.

What I am asking is whether or not your employees are really inspired to give their best efforts at work. Not decent or satisfactory efforts, but their very best efforts. If you don't know the answer, it's time to find out.

I've asked lots of folks this question, and the answers I get are always a bit shocking. The company I founded, Leadership IQ, is both a leadership training and an employee engagement company. Our employee engagement survey is called the Hundred Percenter Index®, and one of the most revealing questions it asks employees to assess is "Working here inspires me to give my best effort."

What we've learned from hundreds of thousands of respondents is that right now, only about 35% of employees say that working at their organization always, or almost always, inspires them to give their best effort. Another 22% are iffy (their scores aren't incredibly low, but they're also not particularly high). And a whopping 45% say, "I am never, or almost never, inspired to give my best effort working here."

This means that if you have 20 employees (who are pretty much like the hundreds of thousands of employees we've surveyed), probably 7 of them are giving their best efforts, 9 of them are nowhere near giving their best efforts, and the remaining 4 are somewhere in the middle.

The business case for addressing this problem should be obvious. If every single person who works for you comes in to work every day charged up, rip roaring, and ready to go, inspired to give her best effort, you and your organization are going to kick some serious butt and crush your targets. But when only 7 out of 20 people feel like that, those targets won't be crushed (gently petted, perhaps, but not crushed).

What's really astounding, though, is that not everyone believes this is a big deal. Some managers (I can't actually call them leaders) think that doing good enough is, well, good enough. I disagree. Think about some of our more recent great innovations: the Internet, Google, iPad, Xbox, portable defibrillators, stem cell research, hybrid cars, protease inhibitors, TiVo, Wi-Fi, genome sequencing, the Large Hadron Collider, Burj Khalifa, Mars rovers, and even seedless watermelons. Are these the creations of people who were doing "good enough"? Or are they the creations of people inspired to give their absolute best effort? I'm going to go with the best effort crowd.

You've chosen to read a book titled *Hundred Percenters*, so you probably don't need a whole lot of convincing that life is more productive, interesting, exciting, and ultimately fulfilling when we're inspired to give our best effort. Hundred Percenters are the people who are inspired to give their best effort (and who have the requisite skills so that effort translates into good results). And when employees with good skills (and this is most people) also give their best efforts, they deliver better quality and service, generate more creative ideas, exhibit more mental toughness, and strive for bigger goals.

Why Isn't Everyone a Hundred Percenter?

There are lots of reasons why people may not be inspired to give their best effort. For example, the past few years have seen some pretty tough economic times that have challenged a lot of people. But that's really more of an excuse, because in spite of those tough times, there are still plenty of organizations whose employees are overwhelmingly giving their best efforts.

Still, we've witnessed a growing trend where organizations and managers use these challenging times as an excuse to ease off practicing real leadership. We've even heard managers snap at demotivated employees with statements like, "Just be glad you have a job" as these managers retreat to their offices and close the doors, shutting out the employees who need them the most. Hopefully it's pretty obvious why that approach doesn't work.

The real reason only 35% of employees are inspired to give their best effort has a lot to do with our leadership. Maybe we hired the wrong people. (We'll address that specifically in Chapter 5, "Hiring for Attitude.") Or perhaps we're just not getting the best from people who might otherwise be so inspired. And then there's a far more disturbing reason.

We recently conducted a study of 207 organizations where we matched engagement survey data with employee performance appraisal results. The annual performance evaluation ratings in our study were provided by the organizations, and the organizations also determined what constitutes a "low performer" and a "high

performer." Employee engagement in these organizations was mea-
sured using the Hundred Percenter Index, and we defined engagement as being inspired to give one's best effort at work. Our study
found that in 42% of the 207 organizations (i.e., 87 companies),
high performers were *less* engaged than low performers. The media
attention that quickly developed around our study results told us
that we'd hit a nerve.

It's disturbing to learn that 42% of high performers are *less*
engaged than low performers. That's why sources including *The New
York Times*, the *Wall Street Journal*, *Forbes*, *Fast Company*, *HR
Executive*, the *Harvard Business Review*, and even Rush Limbaugh
and NPR all reported it. But we need to dig deep if we want to learn
why the situation exists.

The *Wall Street Journal* was the first publication to pick up the
study. Shortly after the article appeared, there followed more than
200 comments (the *Wall Street Journal* lets real people openly comment on articles).

Here are a few of those comments:

> I am involved in a family business that has eight different loca-
> tions, and I have recently seen this scenario playing out in real life.
> Those people who were the top performers in the company 30
> years ago have either left the company or sunk to the level of being
> the low performers. Why? Because they were never recognized for
> the work that they were doing, and they became frustrated with
> having to constantly clean up the low performers' mistakes.

> I concur with this 100%! The incompetent ones are those who are
> given the less responsibility and duties because they can't be
> trusted rather than being fired.

> So characteristic of the healthcare organization I work for: be
> unproductive and surly? Get rewarded with the best shifts and

overtime doing nothing but sitting. Good luck trying to fix it, though. Most people with a clue bide their time, then go elsewhere. You can't change culture overnight.

I work for a company that has actually rewarded mediocrity while the number one performer works the hardest, gets the best customer feedback, goes the extra mile continuously, and is still in the same spot as they started. The end result: an exiting employee who will be picked up by another company and a massive drop in revenue and customer satisfaction for the company that took them for granted. Bad business move for a *sales* company.

This article nails it. I showed it to a few of my productive co-workers and they agreed it was written about us. Things got so bad here we asked for a review from our corporate office HR department. They came and listened to our complaints, and the lazy unproductive had nothing bad to say. The productive hard workers had plenty to say, and we asked to start making everyone accountable. It seemed like an easy request. Wrong. They did nothing. So the slackers are still slacking.

All of these employees, in their own unique ways, are saying, "Yes! We face this problem, and it's why we're so disengaged! Please help us fix it!" Anyone who's had a real job for more than a few years knows the demoralization that comes from being a high performer surrounded by low performers—getting burned out by carrying their load, and resentful over a lack of recognition for your work. This is reality for a whole segment of employees, and it's a very big reason why only 35% of employees are feeling inspired to give their best effort at work.

There are still other reasons why employees might not be inspired to give their best effort. Perhaps they've got uninspiring goals, a lack of performance recognition, or they work for a boss who's closed to discussing employee ideas. But the *Wall Street Journal* comments definitely showcase the fact that creating a demotivating environment for our highest performers is one surefire way to reduce our employees' willingness to give their best effort.

Don't Mistake These Low Performers for High Performers

This book is about creating Hundred Percenters, the employees who give their best effort, and that best effort produces good results. But there are two kinds of low performers you want to make sure you don't mistake for Hundred Percenters.

Bless Their Hearts

Have you ever had employees who really do seem to give their absolute best effort, only that effort doesn't translate into good performance? They try and try and try, but they're just technically incompetent, or they lack the raw intellectual or technical horsepower. These folks are not Hundred Percenters. We call them "Bless Their Hearts."

For anyone who hasn't spent much time in the deep South of the United States, "Bless your heart" is a Southern phrase that basically means "Thanks for trying, but that was so wrong (or dumb or clueless) that my code of Southern gentility prohibits me from talking further, because I might slip and say something really mean." I currently live in the South, but I grew up in the North where instead of "Bless your heart" we said "God love 'em." And by that we meant "I'm sure they meant well, but man alive, that was dumb." And for all my boys in the Bronx and Brooklyn, "That poor bastard" sums it up neatly.

Whether you say "Bless their heart" or "God love 'em" or something else, if you're using these kinds of phrases to describe somebody in your organization who's really trying to do a great job but who just isn't getting the job done right, you're not talking about a Hundred Percenter. You can root for that person every step of the way (and who doesn't want to see a plucky underdog succeed?), but the simple fact is that all the best effort in the world doesn't make someone a Hundred Percenter if his or her performance isn't good.

Talented Terrors

Talented Terrors are the opposite of the Bless Their Hearts. Talented Terrors have the technical capabilities to do a great job, but they just flat-out refuse to put forth their best effort. The root cause may be that they're too lazy to try or too arrogant or too narcissistic to even care. But we can't just call these folks lazy or arrogant or entitled and leave it at that. Talented Terrors have a tremendous negative impact on everyone around them, and they're a big demotivator to other employees who might otherwise be inclined to give their best efforts. That's why we'll cover them in more detail later in the book.

How Do You Make Someone a Hundred Percenter?

Now that we know what Hundred Percenters are (and aren't), the question for leaders becomes, "How do we inspire our people to give their best efforts in our organization?" There are two ways to accomplish this. First, you can lead people to give their best effort. Second, you can give individuals the tools to inspire themselves to give their best efforts.

This book is intended as a road map for leaders, so it might strike you as odd that I even present the second option. You might ask, "Is it even possible for people to inspire themselves to give their best effort?" The answer is yes. In fact, giving folks the tools to inspire themselves is an amazingly powerful path to creating and retaining Hundred Percenters. The concept of self-engagement isn't the topic of this book, but it is the focus of my book scheduled for 2014 publication. In the meantime, visit www.leadershipiq.com for updates.

For the purpose of this book, we'll focus on what leaders can do to inspire employees to give their best effort. For that we're going to turn again to Leadership IQ's Hundred Percenter Index. Our employee engagement survey typically asks around 40 questions to ensure we hit all the top engagement issues that are important in an organization. If your survey asks only 9 questions, or 10 or 12 or 14 questions, it's not enough to help you figure out exactly what makes your unique group of employees tick.

I've run hundreds of regression analyses from similarly sized organizations that show that one group of employees is usually driven by radically different issues than another. For instance, a nurse in a small community hospital in Alabama is likely to have different motivational drivers than a stock trader on Wall Street or a government employee or a soldier in Iraq or a Gen Y programmer in Silicon Valley—just as a commissioned salesperson will have different motivational drivers than will a civil service employee.

Each of these people made radically different career choices, and they all have radically different work schedules, workloads, compensation packages, missions, levels of job risk, etc. So while some of these folks might do their job just fine without a best friend sitting next to them, others might be more motivated to give their best effort by taking on risky projects, and still others by having greater security and predictability.

The Hundred Percenter Index asks up to 40 questions because that's how many questions it takes to really figure out what motivates and inspires a group of uniquely different people. A broad-based diagnosis allows us to then narrow down the data to just the few key factors that inspire the organization's people. This lets us create action items focused specifically on attracting, creating, and retaining Hundred Percenters as they're specifically defined in that organization.

This book was written to address the needs of potentially millions of leaders and organizations, so we needed a list of engagement issues that are pretty common across a wide variety of situations. After culling through hundreds of thousands of survey records, we determined the following 14 survey questions from the Hundred Percenter Index are significant predictors of whether an employee will be inspired to give his or her best effort at work.

1. I think the organization's strategy will make us more successful.
2. My assigned individual goals for this year will help me grow and develop.
3. The work I do makes a difference in people's lives.
4. Constructive feedback from my leader has helped me to improve my performance.
5. My leader holds people accountable for their performance.
6. My leader distinguishes between high and low performers.

7. My leader recognizes my accomplishments with praise.
8. This organization shares its success stories with its employees.
9. When I share my work problems with my leader, he/she responds constructively.
10. My leader removes the roadblocks to my success.
11. This organization hires people who have the right attitude to be high performers.
12. This organization hires people who have the right attitude to fit our culture.
13. Actually practicing this organization's values is critical to my success here.
14. This organization has clearly defined what behaviors are necessary to achieve success here.

Again, when employees give high marks on these questions, they are also very likely to be inspired to give their best effort at work.

You may have noticed that all 14 questions from our engagement survey have a clear path to action. In every case it's easy to figure out what a leader would need to do to address these issues. Asking survey questions about things you can't fix is a big problem for a lot of organizations because every survey question you ask implies a promise that you're going to do something positive with the answer you get. If you don't know exactly what actions will fix a situation, and you ask about it anyway, you're setting the stage for employees to doubt your leadership capabilities. That's when you'll hear employee grumbling that sounds like, "Gee, the boss asked how we felt about these issues, and we all said lousy, and then he didn't even do anything about it."

Other surveys commonly ask questions about whether employees have friends at work and whether they trust their boss. But what if you get low scores on those questions? Obviously, now you need to do something about it. Let's start with the trust issue. Do you know specifically what causes the typical employee to trust the boss? How about what specifically causes your unique employees to trust the boss? And what steps have you taken to validate these issues?

Low scores on a question that asks if employees have a good friend at work don't teach you exactly what steps you need to take to fix the issue. Social networking might improve friendships, but so might more teamwork or less teamwork, or spending more time together or less time together, etc. Or the solution might depend on your unique culture. Bottom line, if you really want to know what's going to work for your folks, you've got to ask about those solutions specifically.

Every question on the Hundred Percenter Index has the solution built right into the question. So when leaders discover an engagement area where there are weaknesses, they know immediately how to fix it with a clear path of action

You can judge how effective your current employee survey is by taking a good look at every question on the survey. Ask yourself, "Do I know exactly what actions will fix this issue?" It's not good enough to be able to guess what might work; you have to know with complete certainty what you will do. If you don't have a definitive answer, the survey question has no value and needs to be eliminated.

The Six Big Themes

If we return to our list of 14 highly predictive survey questions from the Hundred Percenter Index, a breakdown of the questions produces these six underlying themes:

Theme #1: Goals

Let's look at the first three survey questions:

> I think the organization's strategy will make us more successful.
> My assigned individual goals for this year will help me grow
>   and develop.
> The work I do makes a difference in people's lives.

Behind the scenes of every truly great accomplishment is a challenging goal that tried and tested people's beliefs about what was possible. A goal that made people feel they were contributing to achieving something meaningful and significant. Your people want to know "Why is achieving this goal important and meaningful?" and "How will I and others benefit from this goal?" But if you leave them to figure it out all alone, without any help, they'll eventually go looking for another organization that does help them find the sense of purpose they want.

Your talented people will give their best efforts if you give them goals that are inspiring, vivid, and even a bit challenging. In Chapter 1, "Set HARD Goals," you'll learn how to set goals that are Heartfelt, Animated, Required, and Difficult. HARD Goals raise the bar high, excite the brain, and push people hard so they do achieve greatness.

Theme #2: Constructive Feedback

The next two survey questions are:

> Constructive feedback from my leader has helped me to
>   improve my performance.
> My leader holds people accountable for their performance.

People make mistakes, and they sometimes fail to achieve their full potential. This means there will be times when leaders must provide corrective feedback. But most people don't tolerate getting scolded or corrected with a blunt analysis of the problem. And popular softening "tricks" such as "criticize the action, not the person" or "layer the critical feedback with praise to make it sound kinder and gentler" only exacerbate the situation. Equally, there's nothing for employees to learn about how to make performance changes so they do better the next time when the boss vaguely says, "Your performance is terrible; do something about it."

In Chapter 2, "Create Accountability with Constructive Feedback," readers learn a six-step process for delivering tough feedback called IDEALS. The IDEALS technique lowers people's "walls of defensiveness" and prepares employees to hear and assimilate corrective feedback. This gives leaders who might otherwise be hesitant to offer corrective feedback the power to do so effectively. And for any leaders who offer feedback that's so tough it becomes ineffective, this chapter will teach you how to dial it back to deliver feedback that inspires people to give their best effort.

Theme #3: Positive Reinforcement

The next three survey questions are:

> My leader distinguishes between high and low performers.
> My leader recognizes my accomplishments with praise.
> This organization shares its success stories with its employees.

Improving employee performance also depends upon positively reinforcing people when they give their best effort. Our studies show that receiving positive reinforcement is one of the top predictors of achieving really difficult goals. Yet only 39% of employees say their boss does a good job of recognizing and acknowledging their accomplishments.

You'll learn in Chapter 3 that positive reinforcement doesn't mean lavishing praise and rewarding people for menial achievements (like showing up for work on time). Positive reinforcement is a tool to be used with laserlike precision to identify and reward behaviors that truly represent someone's best effort. Readers will see the science of human motivation distilled into a system for providing meaningful, specific, and timely feedback that maximizes motivational impact and encourages higher performance.

Theme #4: Motivators and Demotivators

The next two survey questions are:

> When I share my work problems with my leader, he/she responds constructively.
> My leader removes the roadblocks to my success.

There's a great deal of confusion over what people find most motivating. For example, 89% of managers surveyed believe that money is the biggest reason employees quit. But 91% of employees surveyed say money had nothing to do with their decision to leave an organization. Maybe your people want certain hours, more flexibility, better benefits, or career advancement. And then there are the folks who just want to do their current job without being pushed to climb any higher. And even the best talent can stop giving their best effort when they can't stand their boss or they dislike their coworkers.

There's no such thing as one-size-fits-all when it comes to keeping employees brimming with the level of passion that inspires best efforts. In Chapter 4, "Shoves and Tugs," readers will learn how to identify employee demotivators (Shoves) that cause people to stop giving their best effort and motivators (Tugs) that excite people and inspire them to go above and beyond. I'll share scripted questions and conversations to help you learn what elicits your people's best efforts and discover what drains your employees' enthusiasm and causes them to turn a deaf ear to your leadership.

Theme #5: Hiring for Attitude

The next two survey questions are:

> This organization hires people that have the right attitude to be high performers.
>
> This organization hires people that have the right attitude to fit our culture.

Most leaders and managers already know how to hire people with the right technical skills, but that's no guarantee they're hiring people who are likely to become Hundred Percenters. In Chapter 5, "Hiring for Attitude," readers will learn why hiring success depends upon having a deep understanding of the attitudes that define an organization's success. You'll learn how to ask nonleading interview questions that reveal the truth about attitude, and how to check candidates' responses to those questions against customized Answer Guidelines that teach the Positive Sign and Warning Signal indicators of whether a candidate is a great, good, or poor attitudinal fit for the unique organizational culture.

Theme #6: Walking the Talk

The last two survey questions are:

> Actually practicing this organization's values is critical to my success here.

This organization has clearly defined what behaviors are
necessary to achieve success here.

Not everyone knows what "giving their best effort" really looks
like. In Chapter 6, "Word Pictures," readers will learn how to define
employee performance expectations on three levels: "Needs Work,"
"Good Work" and "Great Work." Word Pictures make it easy for
the people who are invested in reaching a higher level of performance to get there.

Your Leadership Style

When you look at the 14 survey questions that are the top performance predictors, and the six themes that develop from these
questions, you can see that a leader has to *both* challenge employees
and build a deep connection with employees in order to get high
marks. This requires a distinctive leadership style that we call being
a 100% Leader.

For example, consider these employee survey questions:

My assigned individual goals for this year will help me grow
and develop.

Constructive feedback from my leader has helped me to
improve my performance.

My leader holds people accountable for their performance.

This organization has clearly defined what behaviors are
necessary to achieve success here.

Employees who give strong scores on these questions have leaders who challenge them. Giving employees goals that help them

grow and develop necessitates that those goals are going to be challenging. The same applies for holding people accountable or giving constructive feedback. If you're doing those things well, you're challenging your employees.

Similarly, there are questions amongst those 14 that require leaders to build a deep connection with their employees. For example, consider these survey questions:

My leader recognizes my accomplishments with praise.
This organization shares its success stories with its
    employees.
When I share my work problems with my leader, he/she
    responds constructively.
My leader removes the roadblocks to my success.

When employees feel comfortable sharing work problems with the boss, it's because a deep leader–employee connection has been built. Sharing success stories and recognizing employee accomplishments are two ways to build that connection.

I mention these two issues—Challenge and Connection— because these two concepts broadly represent what it takes to inspire people to give their best effort. Two of the most important decisions you make as a leader are how much you want to challenge your folks to give their best effort and how tight an emotional bond you want to build with them. These two decisions determine exactly what kind of leader you're going to be.

After analyzing leaders' performance on these two dimensions, we've been able to "type" the four major styles of leaders, shown in Figure I-1.

If you neither build an emotional bond with your people, nor challenge them, you're an Avoider (you're also not doing much that could be called leading). If you challenge people to give their best

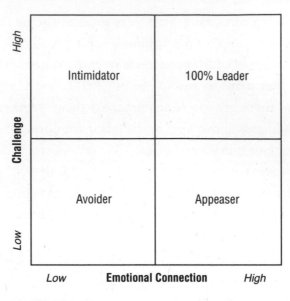

Figure I-1

effort, but you don't create much of a connection, you're an Intimidator. If you connect with your folks, but you don't challenge them all that much, you're an Appeaser. And if you issue great challenges while building intense connections with people, you're the ultra-desirable 100% Leader. (You can take a test at www.leadershipiq.com to see where your current leadership style falls.)

Now, it's nice to know what style of leader you are, but it's even more important to know which style is ultimately the most effective. After all, if being a jerk actually inspired people to give their best effort, who could argue with being a jerk? Here's where the Hundred Percenter Index again becomes useful.

We selected a pool of roughly 25,000 leaders for whom we had engagement survey data and data on budget performance (whether cost or profit centers), employee turnover, employee surveys, and, for a smaller subset, a measure of innovativeness. We then selected the top 10% of performers on budget, turnover, and innovativeness to see what kinds of scores they received on the Hundred Per-center Index.

The top 10% of budget performers were those who either made the most profit or came in most under budget. (In coordination with the respective client organizations, we made every attempt to weed out those who dangerously slashed budgets and, in the process, did serious damage to their departments.) We found, overwhelmingly, that the best performers were 100% Leaders. Looking at Figure I-2, you'll see that some leaned toward Intimidators, as Challenge seemed slightly more important than Connection here, but the numbers weren't significant.

The top 10% of employee turnover performers were those who had the lowest voluntary turnover (essentially, employees who left on their own without being terminated). Again, we found that,

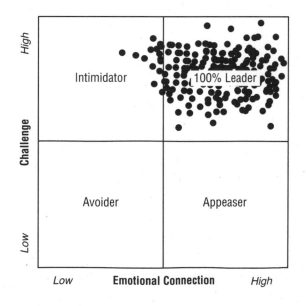

Figure I-2

overwhelmingly, the best performers were 100% Leaders. This time, as you can see in Figure I-3, there were some who leaned toward Appeasers, as Connection was slightly more important than Challenge, but not in significant numbers.

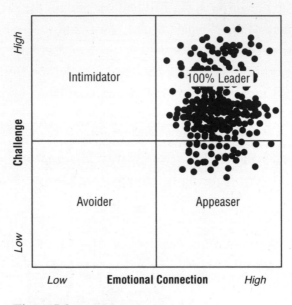

Figure I-3

And the top 10% of performers on innovativeness were determined by the senior leaders at each client organization (they could assess product innovations, service innovations, efficiency innovations, etc.). Yet again, as seen in Figure I-4, the best performers were 100% Leaders. For this factor, Challenge and Connection seemed about equally important.

The results seem pretty clear. If you push people, but you don't seem to care about them, you're not going to be very successful. And if you care about people, but not enough to push them to become Hundred Percenters, you're not going to be very successful. But if you

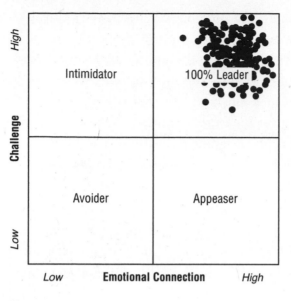

Figure I-4

care enough about your folks to push them beyond what they think they're capable of (i.e., you're a 100% Leader), you will succeed.

The age-old question plaguing leaders is whether it's better to be loved or feared. Our research suggests that while fear doesn't lead to superior results, it's also true that if being loved means you don't push people, that's not so great either. Ultimately, leaders should be loved, but they should be loved for pushing their people to give their best effort, not for coddling or appeasing employees.

Test the Need for Challenge and Connection Yourself

Here's a brief description of what it would be like to work for each style of leader:

Working for the Appeaser. You're given enjoyable assignments; you're allowed to spend most of your time on work that plays to your strengths; your boss gives you lots of positive feedback; your boss seems to care most about making sure you're really happy.

Working for the Intimidator. You're given seemingly impossible assignments; you don't feel like you've got all the skills you need to complete those assignments; when your boss gives you feedback, it's usually pretty harsh and critical; your boss seems to care most about achieving his goals no matter who's with him at the end.

Working for the Avoider. Your boss doesn't really force too many assignments on you; you're not really required to learn new skills; your boss lets you figure out for yourself how you're doing; your boss seems to care most about not getting in your way.

Working for the 100% Leader. You're given really challenging assignments; you're required to learn new skills even in areas you might not consider to be your natural strengths; your boss gives you lots of constructive and positive feedback; your boss seems to care most about pushing you to maximize every ounce of your potential.

We wanted to see how people would evaluate each style, so we asked 3,000 random people (not paying clients) a series of questions about whom they wanted to work for (I'll give you a link to the questions below so you can do this exercise yourself and with your employees).

We asked questions like, "Which leader would you choose if you wanted . . ."

A deeply fulfilling job?
A job you would be proud to tell your children about?

A job where you would grow as a professional?
A job where you would grow as a person?
The greatest chance of career success?
The greatest chance of achieving great things?
To maximize your full potential?

In every single case, more than 70% of respondents chose the 100% Leader. There are exceptions, of course, but generally speaking, people don't want to work for jerks, and they also don't want to be coddled all day.

To be fair, when we asked the question, "Which leader would you choose if you wanted a fun job?" the Appeaser garnered 56% of the votes. It's a deep philosophical decision every leader has to make: Is your job to make work fun or is it to make work fulfilling and enriching and ultimately to position people to achieve great results?

Download the full list of test questions at www.leadershipiq.com and take the test for yourself. If you give the test in a group setting, a fascinating exercise is to have everybody answer the questions and then discuss what motivated the respective choices. What aspects of the 100% Leader or the Appeaser or the Intimidator or the Avoider were most appealing? And did responses change depending on whether the question was about fun or fulfillment or great achievement?

The Current Leadership Style Trend

Recently (from late 2012 to early 2013), 5,211 leaders completed Leadership IQ's online leadership scenario test. Here participants assume the role of CEO at a fictional company and are asked to solve 10 distinct leadership situations, ranging from leading change to managing talented executives with difficult personalities to confronting sacred cows. The test slotted leaders into the four primary leadership styles: Intimidator, Appeaser, Avoider, and 100% Leader. (You can take this free test for yourself at www.leadershipiq.com.)

Here are the results at the time this book went to press:

> Some 39% of leaders currently employ an Intimidating leadership style, typified by seemingly impossible assignments for employees, lots of tough and critical feedback, and an emphasis on short-term bottom-line results with little regard for softer issues like employee motivation, engagement, or turnover.
>
> Meanwhile, only 17% of leaders lean toward the other extreme—an Appeasing style—typified by easy assignments for employees, lots of positive feedback, and an emphasis on employee happiness with little regard for bottom-line results.
>
> And 16% of leaders employ an Avoiding style, neither intimidating nor Appeasing, essentially adopting a laissez-faire (i.e., hands-off) posture with their staff.
>
> And finally, 28% of leaders are finding the ideal mix with a 100% Leader style. This approach involves giving employees challenging assignments that simultaneously drive growth and performance, providing a healthy mix of positive and corrective feedback, and driving bottom-line results by helping employees maximize their full potential.

Interestingly, this percentage of Intimidating leaders is as high as it's been since Leadership IQ started this particular online assessment in 2004. While the Intimidating style is not nearly as effective as the 100% Leader style in producing results from employees, it is a common style to employ (whether consciously or unconsciously) during times of economic stress and fatigue.

Back in 2005 to 2007, however, leaders faced a very different world. Books on "happiness" were all the rage, and many workplaces were focusing on employee strengths rather than weaknesses (i.e., giving people work that they were already good at rather than asking them to develop in new areas). In that context, the Appeaser style was much more popular than its meager 17% today, hitting an all-time high of 32%.

In contrast to these fluctuations, great leadership seems to come with a constancy foreign to the other styles, as the 100% Leaders' 28% share has remained roughly the same over the past eight years (within four percentage points).

Finally, while much has been written about the varying management styles between men and women, when it comes to solving the leadership scenarios, in our test, women were just as likely as men to employ the Intimidating leadership style. Some 40% of men and 39% of women were categorized as Intimidators.

Conclusion

When all your employees are inspired to give their best effort, there's really no limit to what your organization can achieve. This book is a road map to help you create and retain those Hundred Percenter employees.

As we move through the next six chapters, keep these 14 questions from the Hundred Percenter Index firmly in your mind:

1. I think the organization's strategy will make us more successful.
2. My assigned individual goals for this year will help me grow and develop.

3. The work I do makes a difference in people's lives.
4. Constructive feedback from my leader has helped me to improve my performance.
5. My leader holds people accountable for their performance.
6. My leader distinguishes between high and low performers.
7. My leader recognizes my accomplishments with praise.
8. This organization shares its success stories with its employees.
9. When I share my work problems with my leader, he/she responds constructively.
10. My leader removes the roadblocks to my success.
11. This organization hires people that have the right attitude to be high performers.
12. This organization hires people that have the right attitude to fit our culture.
13. Actually practicing this organization's values is critical to my success here.
14. This organization has clearly defined what behaviors are necessary to achieve success here.

The next six chapters will show you how to utilize these 14 questions toward creating a Hundred Percenter workplace where all your people give their best efforts and where those best efforts produce good results.

1

Set HARD Goals

Leadership IQ's Hundred Percenter Index Questions

I think the organization's strategy will make us more successful.

My assigned individual goals for this year will help me grow and develop.

The work I do makes a difference in people's lives.

Introduction

Our goals are one of the few things we truly control in this world. And if you're in charge of other people's goals, to a large degree, you control those as well. The good news is it doesn't require innate talent to set and achieve extraordinary goals. Everyone has the capacity to accomplish virtually anything imaginable. But contrary to what most people think, it's not daily habits or raw intellect or how many numbers get written on a worksheet that decide goal success. Rather, HARD Goals are what excite the brain and push us hard to achieve greatness.

Just think about your own most significant professional or personal accomplishment. Maybe you invented the coolest product in your industry, doubled your company's revenue, got that big promotion, or even lost 30 pounds or ran a marathon. Whatever it was, I bet it resulted from an incredibly challenging, deeply emotional, and highly visual goal. A goal that pushed you outside your comfort zone, forced you to learn new things, and made you feel scared, exhilarated, and 100% committed all at the same time. On that day, when you finally hit your big goal, you felt as fulfilled as you've ever been. Even now, months or years later, just thinking about achieving that goal makes you feel highly satisfied. I'm not talking about some temporary high, such as the one you get from eating chocolate. I mean deep, life-altering, perspective-changing fulfillment.

The overwhelming majority of human beings have the potential to achieve that same kind of Hundred Percenter greatness. They just need some gutsy, challenging goals to help them get there. HARD Goals work because they push us past our comfort zones, challenge our beliefs about what's possible, and force us to learn new skills. HARD Goals stimulate the brain, making us wide awake and aware. And they deliver such an overwhelming sense of empowerment and pride that they leave us no choice but to get started immediately and to never give up.

Most of us already know from our own experiences how effective these kinds of goals are. Yet the majority of managers set employee goals that are small, achievable, realistic, and easy—goals that nudge employees toward complacency instead of driving them toward greatness. It's not just managers and organizations that feel the pain of these inadequate and uninspiring goals. Your employees are suffering too. A Leadership IQ survey found that only 15% of employees strongly agree that their goals will help them achieve great things. And only 13% of employees really believe that their goals this year will help them reach their full potential.

100% Leaders Have Courage

Demanding more of ourselves and each other is scary. Some leaders fear that their employees are already pushed too far. Other leaders subscribe to the religion of Happiology and its slogan of "Don't do today what you can put off until tomorrow." In other cases, organizations throw roadblocks in front of 100% Leaders who otherwise would test their employees' limits. We see this in situations where no goal can be approved until every resource is allocated, every milestone clarified, every assumption tested, every participant vetted, every response anticipated, every market researched, and every skill developed.

We might be afraid of challenges, but, ironically, companies generally don't die because they tackled a challenge that was too big or they pushed themselves too hard. In virtually every major business failure, adhering to the status quo was the cause behind the business's undoing. Kodak didn't meet the challenge when Fuji attacked, nor did Sears when Walmart moved in for the assault. The Big Three automakers have made sticking to the status quo an art form—whether it's union contracts or high oil prices, they never met a tough challenge they couldn't duck or postpone. How many different companies were status quo-ing themselves to death when Google first emerged? Or Amazon? Or Southwest? Or Microsoft?

Or Dell? Or Yamaha? Or Honda? (Please note some of these companies now face significant challenges. So ask yourself: Are they in trouble because they challenged themselves too much or because they became so enamored with their own success that they stopped looking for greater challenges?)

Yes, companies with challenging goals do fail. But it's rarely, if ever, the goal itself that causes the failure. Rather, what our research shows is that the failure occurs in how leaders communicate, execute, and/or resource the goal. What's more, companies with the guts to set challenging goals that are bigger than themselves typically have the cultural constitution to pick themselves up from failure and start again. In addition, our research shows that people who set HARD Goals feel up to 75% more fulfilled than do people with weaker goals.

There's simply no room for adequate goals in the Hundred Percenter workplace. And 100% Leaders have the courage to set HARD Goals.

First, let's take a look at why the goals you're currently setting might be holding your people back from reaching their full potential.

Are SMART Goals Dumb?

Virtually every company sets goals for its employees, and what manager hasn't set a SMART goal (most commonly defined as Specific, Measurable, Achievable, Realistic, and Time-bound)? But when Leadership IQ studied 4,182 workers from 397 organizations to see what kind of goal-setting processes actually help employees achieve great things, we learned that SMART goals often act as impediments to, not enablers of, bold action and actually encourage mediocre and poor performance.

As part of our study, we wanted to identify what aspects of goal setting really predict whether an employee will achieve great things. After all, the purpose of goals isn't to help us achieve mediocre results. Goals are supposed to help us achieve extraordinary results. We wanted to know, for example, if achievable and realistic goals drive people to great achievements, or if greatness comes from having goals that are really difficult and that push us out of our comfort zones.

To answer these questions, we conducted a stepwise multiple regression analysis to discover what kinds of goals are most likely to drive people to achieve great things. Stepwise multiple regression is a statistical technique that predicts values of one variable (e.g., achieving greatness) on the basis of two or more other variables (e.g., whether goals are achievable, difficult, and so forth).

Our analysis revealed eight predictors of whether people's goals were going to help them achieve great things. They are listed here in order of statistical importance:

1. I can vividly picture how great it will feel when I achieve my goals.
2. I will have to learn new skills to achieve my assigned goals for this year.
3. My goals are absolutely necessary to help this company.
4. I actively participated in creating my goals for this year.
5. I have access to the formal training I will need to accomplish my goals.
6. My goals for this year will push me out of my comfort zone.
7. My goals will enrich the lives of others (e.g., customers, the community).
8. My goals are aligned with the organization's top priorities for this year.

A few things should jump out at you here. First, some of the SMART goal characteristics—such as achievable, measurable, and realistic—had no unique predictive power in this analysis. In fact, when we conducted a separate correlation analysis, we found that the question about SMART goals (i.e., "We use SMART goals as our goal-setting process") had no meaningful correlation with employees achieving great things.

The second thing that probably hits you is that in order for people to achieve great things, their goals must require them to learn new skills and to leave their comfort zones. That's something that SMART goals don't allow. Because instead of pushing us toward greatness, SMART goals tell us: "Hold on a minute. Be realistic. Don't push beyond your resources. This needs to be achievable, so just play it safe and stay within your limitations." Here again, using a correlation analysis, we found that the question about achievable goals (i.e., "My goals are achievable with my current skills and/or knowledge") had no meaningful correlation with achieving great things.

Now, having said all that, I want to clarify that SMART goals are not all bad. For instance, there's nothing wrong with having a specific goal. In fact, the more specific our goals are, the more likely we are to achieve them. But if a goal doesn't ask people to learn new skills and to leave their comfort zones, it's not going to drive greatness. SMART goals were a brilliant methodology for the slow-moving, command-and-control 1950s era for which they were created. But in today's fast-moving world that demands constant innovation, they have some flaws. If you're still using SMART goals, don't worry. HARD Goals will allow you to "amp up" your existing goals and push past roadblocks such as "achievable" and "realistic," vastly increasing the likelihood of setting meaningful goals that result in great achievements.

I want to share two more critical insights from our regression analysis. The first is that goals need to be much more than just words on a form. For a goal to drive greatness, that goal has to leap off the page. It has to be so vividly described that we can feel how great it will be to achieve it. Second, a goal has to be bigger than ourselves. We have to identify whose lives will be enriched by our goals. And those goals had better be absolutely necessary (and also aligned with your organization's top priorities), or they aren't going to drive anyone to achieve great things.

Here's how HARD Goals work.

HARD Goals

After years of studying Hundred Percenters and the 100% Leaders who enable them, we've distilled the critical success factors of goal setting into the following methodology:

Heartfelt. We feel an emotional attachment to a goal; it scratches an existential itch.

Animated. Our goal is so vividly described and presented that to not reach it leaves us wanting.

Required. A goal needs to feel as critical to our continued existence as air and water.

Difficult. A goal needs to push us outside our comfort zones and to test our limits.

You'll recognize some of the better-known 100% Leaders by the HARD Goals they've set. The HARD Goal in Abraham Lincoln's Gettysburg Address steeled our resolve to fight so that "government of the people, by the people, for the people, shall not perish from the earth." John F. Kennedy's HARD Goal asked the nation to "commit itself to achieving the goal, before this decade is out, of landing a man on the moon and returning him safely to the earth." Ronald Reagan's HARD Goal demanded "Mr. Gorbachev, tear down this wall!" Winston Churchill's HARD Goal made clear that "whatever the cost may be, we shall fight on the beaches, we shall fight on the landing grounds, we shall fight in the fields and in the streets, we shall fight in the hills; we shall never surrender." But you don't have to be a world leader to issue a HARD challenge. You just have to be willing to push past what's easy—to do what's right.

I'm not a natural runner. For most of my life, I wouldn't run even if chased. But a few years ago, my wife (who used to run cross-country) issued me a HARD Goal of running a marathon. It wasn't easy (each step hurt a little more), it wasn't pretty (imagine a sausage with feet), and it sure as heck wasn't fast (over five hours). I once did a four-hour run on a treadmill (which probably hurt worse than the actual race) as part of my training. I also gave up hours of comfortably sitting on my butt on my couch (and I've got a really comfortable couch) during football season.

On any given day, if you had asked me if sitting on my couch watching TV would make me happier than running, I'd have said yes. And if you had totaled up every one of those days during my two-year training period, my "happiness score" would mathematically tilt in favor of sitting. But when the race was over and the nausea had passed and I could walk again, if you had asked me if I was a better person for running a marathon, had discovered an inner strength, had learned that a lack of natural talent should never be an excuse for avoiding a challenge, had become less fearful of big challenges, and had acquired more character and life lessons to offer my children, I would have resoundingly answered *yes*!

Admittedly, my marathon goal was pretty small compared with the famous HARD Goals mentioned above. We might never find ourselves sitting behind the same desks as Lincoln, Roosevelt,

Kennedy, or Reagan, faced with decisions that affect millions of lives. But every business plan we write represents an opportunity for greatness. And every sales presentation, customer interaction, budget request, and financial approval is a chance for us to push ourselves and our employees toward untold greatness. Sure, we can take the easy way and do only what's minimally required. We can stonewall and hide behind the imposed constraints of achievable and realistic goals and encourage our people to do the same. Or we can set HARD Goals.

Let's get started.

Heartfelt

When Leadership IQ works with organizations to help identify and solve their pain points, one factor we look to identify is: Do employees care about their goals? I've had people look me right in the eye and say, "This goal means nothing to me. It's my boss who cares." And I've lost count of the number of CEOs who've said, "Well, it's our chairman who really feels this goal is important." If people only see a goal through for the boss, the chairman, the board, or just to get a paycheck, they're not going to chase to the far corners of the globe to achieve that goal. And if they hit a road-block, they're probably going to stop even trying. Not having that heartfelt connection, on average, cuts into employee willingness to "give" to a goal by 50%.

Early in my career, I advised seriously troubled organizations (ones teetering on the brink of bankruptcy). One way I tested whether or not a struggling organization had the mettle to launch a successful turnaround was to walk around the front lines and ask employees, "Why do you care if this company succeeds or fails?" If I heard a lot of responses like "Because I'll lose my job" or "I need a paycheck," I knew the company probably wouldn't make it. But if I heard something more heartfelt like "I've poured my heart and soul into this place, and I'm not gonna let it fail" or "Too many people are counting on us" or "Our customers need us to survive," then I knew there was a great shot at a comeback.

Ideally, when you ask your people "Why do you care about this goal?" the response you'll hear is "This goal is my passion, it's what I'm here to do" or even "What I really care about is the finish line. I'm totally pumped to get to the payoff." But all too often leaders and organizations get so hung up on making sure their goal-setting forms are filled out correctly and that each goal translates into a simple number that "analytically" fits a spreadsheet that they forget to ask the single most important question: Do you care about this goal?

Leadership IQ was recently called in to improve employee engagement at a large manufacturing company. The company was trying to push through a lot of operational changes but was getting big-time resistance from the unions. We conducted an engagement survey with the Hundred Percenter Index, and at the end of the survey, we asked a series of open-ended questions including: "Please describe a time in the past few months when you felt really motivated" and "Please describe a time in the past few months when you felt really demotivated."

While delivering the survey feedback to the leadership team, I paused before showing the analysis of those open-ended questions and asked, "Why should the union employees feel a deep emotional connection to the operational changes you're making?" Virtually every leader in the room answered, "Well, because they get to keep their jobs, and we've told them that at least a dozen times!"

Next I showed the team the analysis from the open-ended questions as answered by the union workers. Here's one typical example of what nearly all of the union workers had to say (we have removed some words that could identify the company and individual):

Please describe a time in the past few months when you felt really motivated. "One of my brothers at Local XXX was working on trying to fix a [piece of equipment]. And I had just gone through the certification on this equipment. So when he asked for my help and I solved it with the new skills I had just finished learning, I got really pumped. And he was too. Helping my guys is a real thrill."

Please describe a time in the past few months where you felt really demotivated. "Being threatened with [the loss of] my job every single day."

There were about 1,000 comments that echoed this example. I asked the leaders, "When push comes to shove, whose emotional attachment is going to be bigger: yours or the union brothers'?" The leaders' stunned expressions pretty much gave the answer.

Feeling heartfelt passion for a goal excites the brain and creates a surge of motivation that drives employees to give, give, give toward company goals. The most effective way to determine if your people are emotionally attached to their goals is to ask them. If they answer with "I don't care about this goal, you do" or with "Because if I don't do this I'll lose my job" or with "I need a paycheck" or with the kind of wordless shrug that indicates an "I don't know," it's a clear sign that there's no emotional attachment to that goal and no sense of personal ownership. Something needs to change to get these employees to dig deep into their emotional bank accounts.

One fairly simple way to build a heartfelt connection is envisioning the benefit that achieving the goal will deliver to someone else. Google and Apple are two highly successful companies that make serving something bigger than "me" a crucial part of their corporate philosophies. Google says it very well in its corporate philosophy, which includes a list of "Ten things Google has found to be true." Number one is as follows:

Focus on the user and all else will follow. Since the beginning, we've focused on providing the best user experience possible. Whether we're designing a new Internet browser or a new tweak to the look of the homepage, we take great care to ensure that they will ultimately serve you, rather than our own internal goal or bottom line. Our homepage interface is clear and simple, and pages load instantly. Placement in search results is never sold to anyone, and advertising is not only clearly marked as such, it offers relevant content and is not distracting. And when we build new tools and applications, we believe they should work so well you don't have to consider how they might have been designed differently.

Nearly every company on earth puts the word *customer* or *patient* or *user* or *client* in its mission statement. It looks great embossed on a plaque hanging in the boardroom or lobby, but how many companies actually put it right into their goals? The companies that do are more likely to have employees who make sacrifices to serve the customer, patient, user, and so forth. They're the companies that tend to make the most money over time because they deliver the most value to someone bigger than themselves. They don't sacrifice the customer to immediately increase shareholder value because they know it will come back to bite them. Not only will customers revolt, but employees generally won't go above and beyond for a goal that's only self-serving. But put a name and a face to the beneficiary of your organizational efforts, and you'll find your people go from "I know I need to do this goal" to "Nothing is going to get in my way of achieving this goal."

If you want to build a heartfelt higher purpose into your goals and inspire more Hundred Percenters, make your goals NOBLE. You can use the actual definition of NOBLE, or you can use it as an acronym:

Name a party
Other than ourselves who will
Benefit from this goal
Like customers or
End users

See if you can find the Hundred Percenter who is working toward a NOBLE goal in this story: One day, a man came upon a construction site where three masons were working. He asked the first mason, "What are you doing?" The mason slapped down some mortar and said, "I'm laying bricks." The man then asked the second mason the same question, "What are you doing?" The mason shrugged and said, "I'm putting up a wall." Finally, the man approached the third mason, who was whistling as he worked. Once again, he asked, "What are you doing?" The mason stopped whistling, turned to him with a big smile, and said, "I'm building a cathedral."

Lest you think me a Pollyannaish babe in the woods of bare-knuckled corporate politics, let me offer this thought: if your goal is wrapped in the flag of NOBLE purpose, you're about as politically protected as you can be. If you give a speech launching a new initiative and you can demonstrate how it will be better for customers, then who in his right mind is going to stand up and shout, "To heck with the customers. Let's take the money for ourselves"? (Of course, there are those people who will do exactly that, but they will have politically kneecapped themselves with their narcissism.)

One word of caution: you can't play Machiavellian games and speak of NOBLE goals only to turn around and shaft the people or the causes you promised to serve. That's why so many politicians, even though they've mastered the feigned indignation of champions fighting for something bigger than themselves, are so distrusted. They talk a good game, but the Lincolns among them are few and far between.

Are Enemies NOBLE?

Most CEOs won't admit it, but having an enemy is fun. (In sports we call them rivalries and they're essential to ratings and revenue.) Having someone to benchmark against gets our competitive juices flowing and can feel like a NOBLE goal ("We're not focused on ourselves; we're focused on crushing those other people over there"). But while competing against mortal enemies can elevate our performance, there are two dangers. First, beating a competitor is simply not as motivating as serving a more NOBLE aim. The second danger is more practical: When you've beaten the enemy, who do you fight next? Or, put another way, where do you go when you get to number one?

Finally, don't underestimate the power of an extrinsic incentive, where you help employees develop a heartfelt connection to the payoff. Despite all the hoopla about how the only reason to do something is because you love doing it, some goals just don't offer that possibility. In these cases, there's absolute power in focusing on the payoff. Intrinsic or personal motivators are preferable, but if the only thing that's going to inspire someone to move heaven and earth to reach a goal is the vision of the payoff, use it.

Animated

Animating a goal creates a lasting visual image that helps sear the goal into our brains. It makes a goal so compelling, motivating, inspiring, and necessary that your employees will say, "I am going to sacrifice whatever is asked of me to achieve this goal." It all works because of a concept called "Pictorial Superiority Effect," whereby if we can imagine a goal, and really picture that goal, we're more likely to process, understand, and embrace it. In fact, when we hear only information, our total recall is about 10% when tested 72 hours later. Add a picture, and that number shoots up to 65%.

We're all familiar with Martin Luther King Jr.'s speech where he stood on the steps of the Lincoln Memorial and said, "I have a dream . . ." From his words that followed, it's as if we can actually see the red hills of Georgia and the sons of former slaves and the sons of former slave owners sitting down together at the table of brotherhood. It's a goal so powerfully animated that it sends shivers down the spine of anyone listening to it. It's a goal that makes us care and want to be a part of making it happen, even if we're hearing the speech decades later.

But now imagine that instead of the "I have a dream" speech we all know, Dr. King had articulated his goal something like this: "Our goal should be that within the next 30 years, the incidence of hate crimes will be reduced by 63%, and the percentage of minorities living below the poverty line will be no higher than the percentage for any other racial group." Stated this way, it's not exactly a goal that makes you want to jump up and get started. Nor is it very memorable.

An animated goal builds an immensely powerful attachment that helps people experience the goal (albeit in their minds) long before they achieve it. And an animated goal also allows us to simulate our goal mentally so that we can work out any logical problems and uncover any hidden land mines (before we hit them in real life).

Parenthetically, the most useful aspect of SMART goals typically has been the M (measurable). You'll find as you animate your goals that you'll be making your HARD Goals measurable. But you won't just be making them numerically measurable (although that's a key component); you'll also be making them behaviorally and emotionally measurable.

Not everyone is a natural at expressing vivid imagery. Here are some specific tools that will help animate your goals and improve their inspirational quotient.

Picture in Your Mind's Eye

Whether we're talking about the kind of visualization that helps elite athletes perform under pressure or the guided imagery used by cancer patients to destroy their illness, the power of imagery has been documented in countless studies. A study in the *British Journal of Cancer* comparing two groups of female cancer patients found that patients who used imagery were more relaxed and had a higher self-rated quality of life during chemotherapy than patients who didn't use imagery. The imagery patients also had enhanced lymphokine-activated killer cytotoxicity, higher numbers of activated T-cells, and reduced blood levels of tumor necrosis factor, which loosely translated means they seemed healthier than the group not using imagery. Additionally, a study reported in *The Sport Psychologist* found that mental training techniques, including imagery, improved competitive triathlon performance.

Visualization, or imagery, taps into the imagination and encourages a mental rehearsal of the feelings of joy and satisfaction that beating the odds and reaching our HARD Goals will bring. This strengthens our emotional attachment to goal outcome and increases our Hundred Percenter drive to push past all obstacles in order to reach those goals. Employees who are given a strong visual image of what the achievement of a goal will look and feel like will be motivated to access everything they've got, including untapped potential, to make that vision real.

Developing an animated description of a goal requires some mental stretching. Imagine what it will be like when you hit that HARD Goal. Describe what you see, and strengthen the specificity of your visualization with questions such as: How does it feel to have achieved this goal? What are the numbers like? Who's saying what to whom? And share it all with everyone who is part of making that goal happen. You want that future moment to feel so real that when folks are done visualizing it they feel disappointed that the moment is gone. That's what will drive them to make all that great stuff happen for real.

Your visualization should address the actual outcomes of achieving the goal, the necessary steps toward making it happen, and the emotions involved in the entire process.

Outcomes

What specifically was achieved? Outcomes include whatever metrics were achieved, but instead of just saying, "Our project came in a month ahead of schedule," use visual language to help employees look into the future and see the specific outcomes that you'll achieve. For example: "Our project was submitted on March 13, which was 27 days ahead of schedule. We saved 8 of those days in the design phase, because unlike our past projects, we started on time and we made our spec document deadline nonnegotiable. (It took an all-nighter, but it set the tone for the rest of the project.) We saved another 12 days during coding because we held a code-jam with 3 days off-site locked away doing nothing but coding and talking about coding (and eating pizza and drinking coffee). The other 7 days we saved . . ." You get the idea.

The visualizations of your HARD Goal outcomes will have far greater impact if you use absolute numbers instead of percentages. For example, rather than saying, "We came in 10% under budget," say, "We saved $873,000." Here's an interesting discovery we made that explains why absolute numbers are preferable. During a six-month period, we tracked over 2,000 managers, all of whom made New Year's resolutions to lose weight. Not a whole lot of weight was actually lost. But the people who expressed their weight-loss goals in absolute terms (e.g., lose 13 pounds) lost roughly four times more weight than those who expressed their goals in percentages (e.g., lose 5%).

Actions

In the 1930s, Walt Disney Studios came up with the idea of story-boarding its animations as a way to detail the actions that made up the completed films. 100% Leaders use a verbal form of story-boarding to outline the actions that will bring a HARD Goal to life. It may not be quite as captivating as a favorite Disney movie, but when employees are given an animated presentation of the blow-by-blow steps they will take to achieve a goal, they will be more inspired to achieve that goal.

Here's an example of a leader who didn't do a very inspirational job of animating the actions required to achieve a goal: "This is going to be our best quarter ever, but in order to get there, we've got to run our meetings more efficiently."

This certainly sounds hopeful, but it doesn't tell the employees what they'll actually be doing.

Here's how a 100% Leader might express a more animated vision of the action needed to achieve that same goal: "As of this moment, we're done with meetings that eat up time and produce minimal results. Prior to every meeting, you will be receiving longer agendas than you have in the past. Everyone is responsible for knowing the information and coming to the meeting 100% prepared. We won't be stopping or backtracking for anyone to catch up. We'll start with a Statement of Achievement so we know exactly what we're all there to accomplish. That leaves us with deciding who will do the tasks at hand and how, at which point the meeting will end."

Feelings

I suspect the Wright brothers had a pretty clear picture of what it would feel like to fly before they succeeded in building an airplane that left the ground. That feeling of success, before it is achieved, is one of the main drivers behind Hundred Percenter effort. You can't expect your people to keep reaching for a goal if they have no idea what achieving it will feel like. Everyone has something to gain from bringing a HARD Goal to life. Pinpoint what it is and help your people visualize how great that moment of success will feel.

Animated goals are all about imagination and creativity. We've had clients throw goal-achievement parties for their employees at the launch of a HARD Goal to help cement the imagery of the upcoming yearlong challenge. Other clients have premarked company calendars to "track" future achievements. Some clients have distributed mock articles that looked as if they were written up in *USA Today* to "document" future achievements. Others introduce a HARD Goal by giving awards and a formal presentation—as though employees have already achieved their goals.

Our brains remember pictures more than they do words, so make your HARD Goals as graphic as possible. You don't need to be a professional speechwriter or artist to create a goal filled with imagery. Just write what you feel and back it up with actual pictures, drawings, or a collage or vision board. Whatever route you choose, capture the specific elements of your goal, such as size, color, shape, distinct parts, setting, background, lighting, emotions, and movement.

Required

Logically, we all know that the basic rule of most goals is: exert some effort now and get some benefits in the future. For example, if I said to you, "Give me $100 today and I'll give you $170 two months from now," you'd probably take the deal. But what if the payoff is six months from now, or a year, or even five years? Suddenly the cost of giving up that $100 starts to weigh on you. You're not sure if giving up the status quo (your $100) is really worth it. There's no motivation to act, let alone act with urgency, to achieve greatness. This is one of the reasons goal procrastination (which kills far too many goals) starts to set in.

But give the brain a taste of how good achieving a goal will be, and suddenly that goal becomes as necessary to our survival as air or water. The sacrifices and discomforts don't even register, or, if they do, they feel worth it. We take ownership of that goal, and we can't wait to get started on it. It's called the endowment effect, a psychological bias discovered by Richard Thaler and inspired by Amos Tversky and Daniel Kahneman. It basically says that people place a higher value on objects they own than on objects they don't own.

A great experiment that demonstrates the endowment effect was conducted by Irwin Levin, from the University of Iowa, and Marco Lauriola, from the Sapienza University of Rome. In the experiment, college students in Iowa and Italy were given the task of building their own pizzas by selecting from a menu of 12 ingredients. In the American version, the students were divided into two groups: an Adding Condition and a Subtracting Condition. In the Adding Condition, subjects started with a description of a "basic" cheese pizza with no extra ingredients and were asked to select additional toppings, such as mushrooms, peppers, pineapple, pepperoni, and so forth, for 50 cents each. In the Subtracting Condition, subjects started with a "super" pizza with all 12 ingredients and were told that the price would be reduced by 50 cents for each topping they subtracted.

Both groups were told they should add or remove as many ingredients as they wanted until they got their preferred pizzas. The Italian version of the experiment was basically the same, but some ingredients were adapted to Italian tastes (for example, pepperoni and pineapple were replaced by Italian hot sausage and Italian vegetables), and the Italian students were also asked to choose ingredients for a salad.

The Subtracting Condition is like taking ownership of the pizza. You've mentally pictured this pizza with all of its ingredients, and as far as your brain is concerned, that's your pizza, right there. If somebody tries to take those ingredients away, your brain is going to say, "Hey, those are my peppers, pepperoni, and sausage!" Even if you don't really love peppers or sausage, your brain is saying, "Those are mine, I own them," and thus is a lot less willing to let go of them. But in the Adding Condition, all you really own is the basic cheese pizza. Those extra ingredients are not "owned" by your brain; you haven't pictured them on your pizza yet, so you don't care as much if they end up on your pizza or not.

In Iowa, students in the Adding Condition ended up with only 2.7 ingredients on average. But the Subtracting Condition students, who mentally owned all of the ingredients and thus were less willing to give them up, averaged about 5.3 ingredients. If you started with the "super" loaded pizza and had to subtract ingredients, you would spend about $1.29 more for your pizza than people who started with just a cheese pizza. The Italian experiment showed the same thing, and even on their salad choices, if students started with the loaded salad, they ended up with twice as many toppings.

Beyond the fact that I really love pizza, what does this all mean? Basically, if you can get your employees to take mental ownership of a goal (like that super pizza), then they will own that goal. If anyone or anything, such as procrastination, tries to steal that goal from them, that sense of ownership will trigger an automatic response in the brain that says, "No way. I've already seen, felt, and smelled what it is like to have this goal. Nothing is going to take this away from me." Because of the endowment effect, the goal becomes required, and your employees are going to be happy and even eager to go above and beyond to maintain possession of that goal.

An easy place to start making HARD Goals required is the Cutting-in-Half technique that quickly breaks down long-term goals into what specifically needs to get done today. Knowing that the daily accomplishments required by Cutting-in-Half determine our eventual goal success creates an ongoing sense of urgency to stay focused on achieving big goals.

Cutting-in-Half

The first step in Cutting-in-Half is to take an objective long view of your HARD Goal and approximate its end date. Some goals are more naturally time-bound than others, but as accurately as you can, estimate the time frame in which the goal will be completed. Cutting-in-Half works with any time frame, but to keep things simple, let's assume your HARD Goal will take one year to accomplish.

Now cut that time frame as follows:

Six months. What do I have to accomplish in six months in order to stay on track for that big one-year goal?

90 days. What do I have to accomplish in the next 90 days to reach that six-month mark?

30 days. What do I have to accomplish in the next 30 days to reach that 90-day mark? (Of course, 30 days is not actually half of 90, but it's easier to think in terms of one month than 45 days, so it's a simple little useful heuristic here.)

Today. What do I need to accomplish today to stay on track for the 30-day mark?

Difficult

The idea that difficult goals lead to better performance seems counterintuitive, but decades of research support it. Difficult goals demand our attention and engage the brain. And with that extra neurological horsepower comes enhanced performance. But it's a challenge to create goals that perfectly hit the sweet spot of difficulty—that place where people feel right between "so hard I want to quit" and "so easy I can't be bothered to try."

Psychology professors Edwin Locke and Gary Latham, who could be called the fathers of goal-setting theory, radically altered how we think about goals. In the mid-1950s, it was thought that task difficulty had an inverse curvilinear relationship with performance. In other words, when goals were either too easy or too hard, people didn't perform well, but when goals were moderately difficult, people performed their best (see Figure 1-1).

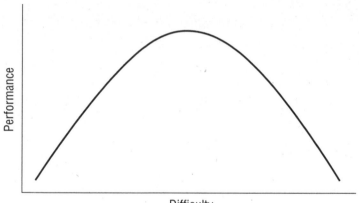

Figure 1-1 It was once believed that task difficulty had an inverse curvilinear relationship with performance.

However, as Locke and Latham refined the science in the 1960s and '70s, they discovered a positive linear relationship between difficulty and performance (see Figure 1-2).

In study after study, they found that, on the whole, as the difficulty of the goal increased, performance also increased, provided that the goal was specific. You couldn't just tell people to "do their

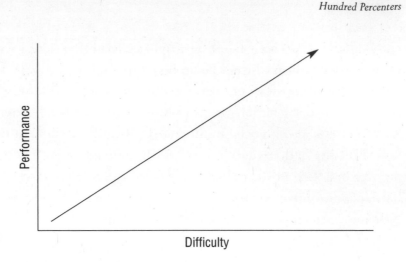

Figure 1-2 Locke and Latham discovered a positive linear relationship between difficulty and performance.

best" on a really difficult goal, because when faced with this bit of management pabulum, people chose not to do their best. But make the goal specific and hard, and you get results. Certainly performance could be expected to drop when the true limits of one's ability are reached. But pushing people that hard is a pretty rare occurrence in the real world of work where "good enough" is more common than "great."

We conducted our own study to see how people really feel about HARD Goals. We asked 4,200 of our subscribers a series of questions, including the following, and asked them to rate their answers on a 7-point scale:

"My boss pushes me harder than I would push myself."
"I will have to exert extra effort to achieve my assigned goals for this year."
"I will have to learn new skills to achieve my assigned goals for this year."

Guess what? Our regression analyses showed that as scores on these questions went up, so did scores on the following four outcome questions:

"I consider myself a high performer."
"The work I do makes a difference in people's lives."
"I recommend this company to others as a great place for people to work."
"I recommend my boss to others as a great person to work for."

Our study shows that bosses who push employees harder than the employees would push themselves—who assign goals that require extra effort and skills development to succeed—have employees who like the boss and the company and who feel better about themselves and the work they do.

One reason these sentiments prevail is that HARD Goals instill confidence. Nobody would give HARD Goals to a moron. You'd give HARD Goals only to someone who had a shot at hitting them. So, by extension, if your boss gives you a HARD Goal, he or she must believe you can achieve it. That is another way of the boss saying, "I believe in you; I trust you; you're the right person for this job." (You might be tempted to argue that your boss is just sadistic, but if HARD Goals also make you feel good about yourself, a sadist would avoid HARD Goals for fear of improving your self-esteem.)

Another reason for the positive feedback is that HARD Goals convey that your work is important. No one would spend the time or energy to create HARD Goals for work that was non-value-added (i.e., dumb, wasteful, and so forth): "You know that report we produce that no one ever reads? That only gets produced because a hundred years ago the founder used to like to verify the calculations from his abacus; you know the report I mean? Well, let's convene a team with a goal of making this dumb report take 10 minutes instead of 20 to produce. It will test the very limits of kindergarten math and data-entry typing, but let's go for it!" Please.

How Difficult Is Difficult?

Please don't misunderstand me. I'm not saying you can't create a goal that's so impossible that it becomes demotivating. Of course you could set such an absurd goal (and every so often we run across a truly impossible, and thus demotivating, goal). Rather, what I'm saying is that we have less to fear from goals that are too hard than we do from goals that are not hard enough. Why? Because there is such an enormous headwind pushing against anyone who tries to create really "super-difficult" goals (let alone goals that might be "too difficult") that they're just not very common.

So how hard should you make your goals? Notwithstanding all the great studies that have been done, in the world outside of the laboratory, estimating the difficulty of a goal remains challenging. So here's a quick test to help you figure out if your HARD Goals are hard enough. Start by assessing the goals you've assigned in the past year (they can be annual goals, project goals, or specific assignments).

> *Test #1.* Ask your employees what new skills (if any) they
> had to learn to achieve these goals.

If they aren't learning all sorts of new skills, then your goals are probably not hard enough. Try making your goals 30% harder and evaluate again in three months. Otherwise, if employees have learned a lot, move on to Test #2.

> *Test #2.* Ask your employees if, at the outset, they knew they
> could achieve these goals.

HARD Goals are scary and force us to question our abilities. So if your employees knew they could accomplish the goals before they even started, try making your goals 20% harder and evaluate again in three months.

The Universal Test: Pay Close Attention

The previous tests are designed based on our experience advising thousands of leaders. But the most important experience is really your own. Watch and interact with your employees. See where they're breaking down, look for signs that they're really sweating to accomplish these goals, and be hypervigilant for cleverness and innovation. If you pay enough attention, you should be able to tell if your people are pushing or just coasting.

Applying HARD Goals

HARD Goals can be applied to just about anything. Here's one way to get started.

Career-Focused HARD Goal

Say that as part of an employee career-mapping conversation, you want to discuss creating a career-focused HARD Goal. The following questions hit all four facets of HARD Goals and make employees active participants in bringing their HARD Goals to life. (Note: For purposes of this example, I've put Animated in front of Heartfelt, and Difficult in front of Required, so you can more easily see the logic flow.)

Animated. Think about where you want your career to be, and describe to me exactly what you're doing (what kind of work, who you're working with, what your days look like) one year, three years, and five years from now.

Heartfelt. Describe at least three reasons why you want this goal (the reasons can be intrinsic, personal, and/or extrinsic).

Difficult. What are the three to five most important skills you'll need to develop to achieve this goal? How will you develop those skills?

Required. What do you need to have accomplished by the end of the next six months to keep on track toward achieving this goal? What about by the end of the next 90 days? The next 30 days? What's one thing you can accomplish today?

Notice how the Heartfelt, Animated, Required, and Difficult elements breathe added life into a usually dry conversation? The Animated question asks the employee to develop a crystal-clear picture of where he is headed. You won't get standard stock answers; the employee will really have to think about where he wants to go.

The Heartfelt question checks to see if that animated picture is grounded in deep desire. Consider, for example, an employee whose future picture involves aspirations to be a manager. If you ask, "Why?" and the employee says, "Because I want more autonomy and the freedom to work more independently," you've just discovered a critical disconnect. You know darn well that if autonomy and independence are your drivers, being a manager, where everyone in the world is peppering you with questions and orders, is the last place you should be. Armed with this information, you can now have a deeper conversation with the employee to envision a career map that will actually meet her underlying needs and ensure a future that brings ongoing fulfillment and high engagement.

The Difficult question ensures the employee will grow and develop, introducing a level of challenge that drives motivation. It also critically analyzes the gap between the employee's current skills and any new skills needed to achieve this career goal. The Difficult question also eliminates any notions of entitlement that employees may have in which the only requirement to getting ahead is staying employed. It strongly reinforces the idea that we all have to keep growing and developing if we want to succeed.

The Required question makes clear how even long-term goals have urgent steps we must work on today. This prevents the phenomenon where employees procrastinate pursuing their goals and wait until the last minute to take action.

HARD Goals and Engagement

Effective goals drive greatness. But our research also shows that employees who have HARD Goals are significantly more engaged than employees who have other kinds of goals. Among our study findings are these:

People who answered Always (or Almost Always) to the question "I can vividly picture how great it will feel when I achieve my goals" had 49% higher employee engagement than people who answered Never (or Almost Never).

People who answered Always (or Almost Always) to the question "I have access to any formal training that I will need to accomplish my goals" had 57% higher employee engagement than people who answered Never (or Almost Never).

People who answered Always (or Almost Always) to the question "My goals for this year will push me out of my

comfort zone" had 29% higher employee engagement
than people who answered Never (or Almost Never).
People who answered Always (or Almost Always) to the
statement "My goals are aligned with the organization's
top priorities for this year" had 75% higher employee
engagement than people who answered Never (or
Almost Never).

Conclusion

Virtually all managers set goals for their employees, but often those
goals don't work.

The goal-setting methodologies that we've used for decades
(such as SMART goals and others) don't lead to employees achieving great things. If you want to set goals that inspire people to
achieve great things, those goals have to be:

Heartfelt. They exist to serve something bigger than
    ourselves.
Animated. They're so vividly described and presented that to
    not reach them would leave us wanting.
Required. These goals are as critical to our continued
    existence as air and water.
Difficult. They're so hard they'll test every one of our limits.

HARD Goals make people stronger, more courageous, and
more confident to go after even bigger and better things. That's
why successful people are always making news for achieving extraordinary success again and again. They've done it before, and they
know they can do it again.

HARD Goals force us to push beyond previously conceived self-limitations (and procrastination) by making us want to achieve more than just the status quo. Remember your high school or college physics class and Newton's First Law of Motion? "An object at rest tends to stay at rest, and an object in motion tends to stay in motion with the same speed and in the same direction unless acted upon by an unbalanced force." Apply that law to your employees and they'll keep doing what they're doing, unless you give them HARD Goals to get them excited about doing more.

2

Create Accountability with Constructive Feedback

Leadership IQ's Hundred Percenter Index Questions

Constructive feedback from my leader has helped me to improve my performance.

My leader holds people accountable for their performance.

Introduction

In the real world, mistakes happen. Whether you're coaching an NFL team in the Super Bowl or leading the intensive care unit in a hospital, someone is going to make a mistake or deliver subpar performance.

100% Leaders aren't afraid to constructively critique employee performance when warranted. But they understand there's a fine balance between making corrections that do nothing, corrections that push good employees to Hundred Percenter performance, and corrections that push good employees to stop trying and send them barreling out the door. No one welcomes a humiliating scolding. It makes most people defensive, and once the walls of defensiveness spring up, the chances of someone improving drop into the negative digits.

When good employees make mistakes, whether they are executing HARD Goals or going about their day-to-day performance, they usually are aware that things didn't go right. It might be conscious or subconscious, but in most cases, they know on some level they messed up. (Getting people to come to terms with errors and admit them outright may involve a more psychologically sophisticated approach, but we'll get to that in a minute.) The thing to remember is that chances are good that when your best people mess up, they have already spent some time sweating out their feelings of lousy self-worth. They are already thinking about the repercussions they may face. They don't need you to make them feel bad; they are already doing a good job of that on their own.

Ultimately, your good performers—your Hundred Percenters and those with the potential to become Hundred Percenters—want to move forward from their mistakes and redeem themselves. What they do need from you is guidance on why the errors happened, how to correct the errors, and how to keep the same errors from happening again. And through it all, they want to be treated with respect. After all, these folks have a history of good or promising performance. Mistake or no mistake, that does count for something.

100% Leaders aren't Appeasers, who make corrections that send a feel-good message about employee error, any more than they are Intimidators, who send folks running away in tears over harsh reprimands. The whole purpose of constructive feedback is to get the people who made the errors to see and understand their mistakes, and to care enough to do what it takes to not make those same mistakes again. 100% Leaders give feedback using a technique called the IDEALS script, which doesn't translate to being a good guy or a bad guy; it's just effective. 100% Leaders know that feedback is not about being nice, and it's not about being nasty; it's about getting folks to willingly listen and assimilate and to act accordingly.

The IDEALS tool helps correct errors and inspires Hundred Percenter effort. However, the human defense mechanism has been honed over thousands of years, and folks have developed an impressive array of ways to avoid accountability when things go wrong. So before you approach employees about admitting to and correcting mistakes, it's imperative to understand the barriers you might have to first break down.

When you hear justification for errors such as, "I never got the memo that said I had to do that" or "I would have had it done if Joe had finished his part of the paperwork" or "I wasn't sure I knew how to use that program, and I was afraid of messing things up" or "I know what I need to do, but there's no way I'll be able to do it all," what you're hearing is Denial, Blame, Excuses, and Anxiety. These are the stages that lead up to Accountability.

Some people accept constructive feedback readily no matter how it's presented. They take responsibility for whatever they did that was subpar, and they do whatever it takes to elevate their future performance. These people are in the Accountability stage—no excuses, no finger-pointing, no denial, and no freaking out. But most folks aren't quite there yet; they're in one of the lower levels of the Stages of Accountability.

We've observed that, besides Accountability, there are four typical reactions to receiving corrective feedback: Denial, Blame, Excuses, and Anxiety. These reactions tend to follow a certain logical flow. For example, Denial begets Blame, which then evolves into Excuses, which is followed by Anxiety. Does everyone evolve through these Stages of Accountability in perfect order? Of course not. People can jump back and forth between the stages. They may never enter Denial but spend most of their days in Anxiety or Excuses; they may even have situational-specific reactions (e.g., certain feedback engenders Blame, whereas other feedback is met with Accountability). But as you can see in Figure 2-1, there is a natural logic to the progression of these stages that is useful to understand.

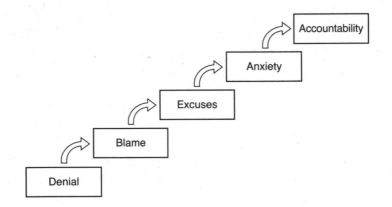

Figure 2-1 Stages of reaction to critical feedback

The opposite of Accountability tends to be Denial. If you've ever heard people say, "That rule doesn't apply to me" or "My performance was just fine" (when it clearly wasn't), you've witnessed Denial. These are folks who are so defensive and walled-off, or their egos are so fragile, that they're simply not ready for feedback. They are, in effect, saying, "There's no problem; my performance was absolutely fine. If you don't like the results, that's a problem with your judgment, not my performance."

Once you've pierced the veil of Denial, people often exhibit Blame. Blame is the unspoken acknowledgment that constructive feedback is warranted (i.e., the outcomes were subpar) coupled with an unwillingness to admit any personal fault. You'll hear things like "Okay, results weren't perfect, but if you want to know where the problem is, go talk to Accounting about why they didn't get the right data to my team before the deadline." Whenever you hear an admission of subpar results followed by someone else's name (or department), you're hearing Blame. (Note: This example presumes you're not in, and don't control, Accounting.)

After Blame comes Excuses. An Excuse is an admission of subpar results plus an admission of fault that is coupled with a host of extenuating factors that no normal human could possibly have overcome. Unlike Blame, it won't be another person or department that gets thrown under the bus but rather your servers, procedures, phone systems, and the like. "I didn't get the message" or "The server crashed just as I finished the report" or "We ran out of supplies" are all commonly uttered variations of Excuses.

After Denial, Blame, and Excuses, the final stage before Accountability is often Anxiety. Here, the actual subpar performance and culpability have been fully acknowledged, but the person lacks the readiness to move forward and improve future performance. People in Anxiety say things like, "There's no way we'll finish in time" or "We've tried to fix this before, and it just didn't work." These folks understand and acknowledge that they're the ones who need to improve, but they lack confidence (they're often freaked out) that they'll be able to make the required improvements.

There's a lot of psychology behind why people try and fall back on Denial, Blame, Excuses, and Anxiety instead of just doing what's asked of them. But you don't need to climb inside your employees' heads to bring them up to Accountability. The 100% Leader shuts down Denial, Blame, Excuses, and Anxiety with a conversation that we call the IDEALS script—a two-way dialogue focused only on the critical feedback. The IDEALS script works no matter where in the Stages of Accountability employees may be. (After we learn the IDEALS script, we'll return to these Stages of Accountability and tie everything together.)

IDEALS for Delivering Constructive Feedback

Most people get defensive when unchecked and random constructive feedback comes their way. They shoot up invisible walls that block out anything difficult or unpleasant to hear. When this total shutdown happens, it typically pushes people in the opposite direction of Hundred Percenter effort; mistakes go uncorrected and are usually repeated. The 100% Leader follows the IDEALS script—a six-step process that allows constructive feedback to penetrate even the most unwilling of ears and that keeps people motivated during and after the feedback is delivered.

IDEALS stands for

Invite them to partner
Disarm yourself
Eliminate blame
Affirm their control
List corrective feedback
Synchronize your understanding

When all six steps are applied collectively, the IDEALS technique generates a domino effect that knocks down, and keeps down, the walls of defensiveness. The result: employees who are open to change and who have a clearer picture of how to reach their full Hundred Percenter potential.

Let's take a look at how IDEALS works to keep employees feeling safe, open, and receptive to constructive feedback.

Invite Them to Partner

Katy is the head of nursing for a small hospital. She recently toughened up on some personnel issues, including a new dress code that requires nurses to wear an assigned identifying color. The new dress-code policy was created to address an increase in complaints from patients who confused nurses with other staff due to the mishmash of colors being worn.

One member of her team, Jill, is a talented nurse, but despite Katy's clear presentation of the new dress code, Jill still sometimes comes to work wearing the wrong color. Whenever Katy questions Jill on the issue, she hears only lame excuses such as, "I forgot."

If Katy had her way, she'd say something like, "Jill, pull your head out of your posterior and pay attention. I want the behavior to stop. End of discussion." However, aside from the dress-code issue, Jill is a good nurse. Katy also knows that while it might feel momentarily good to unload her anger on Jill, it would only make Jill defensive. This would eliminate any chance of solving the problem and helping Jill reach her Hundred Percenter potential.

The only way Katy will get Jill to change is to approach her non-confrontationally. She needs to invite Jill to partner in a dialogue. The classic formulation of this invitation goes as follows: "Would you be willing to have a conversation with me about [insert issue here]?"

Katy's invite to Jill can be as simple as, "Jill, would you be willing to have a conversation with me about the new dress code?" Katy's invitation to partner in conversation (directly stated in a sincere and nonthreatening tone) lets Jill know that the meeting isn't going to be a love and praise fest, but that it won't be a yelling and blame session either.

The invitation to partner in dialogue also expresses an open-ness to hear the other side of the story. This does not mean Katy is inviting Jill to give all sorts of excuses. In this particular instance, Jill has been told by a number of patients that the new dress code looks clinical and makes them feel more depressed. Jill loves her job, especially her patients, and she really wants to be a Hundred Percenter, but she's too timid to talk to Katy about the negatives she perceives in the new dress code. To please her patients, Jill has been hiding behind what she knows are terrible excuses. This infor-mation is beneficial for Katy to hear and sheds light on a potential issue that may need to be further explored.

Let me be clear: I'm not saying that there is always another side to the story. Heck, I'm not even saying there's regularly another side. But every so often, if you view the other person as a partner rather than as an adversary, you might discover a bit of informa-tion that is really going to help you achieve your desired goals.

Face-to-face is the preferable approach when inviting an employee to partner in a dialogue. Not only do the words convey a nonconfrontational situation, but when people hear a relaxed tone and see friendly body language, it enhances their receptivity to the invitation.

In some cases, if the preexisting relationship is strong enough, you can send your invite to partner in a dialogue via e-mail or even in a text message. Whatever method you choose to extend the invite, the main thing is to erase all signs of intimidation from your words. You want to send a clear message that this is just two people sitting down to exchange information in order to come to a resolution.

Most people naturally feel safer and perform better when they are given choices, so you can provide some options about when the talk will take place. This can easily be done by following up your invite with a statement such as, "Do you want to talk now, or would you prefer to wait until after lunch?" While, in theory, you're offering the employee a choice, the catch is that you wrote all the options based upon what you need and want.

Note: There is one caveat to the invitation-to-partner technique. Beware of using the technique if you have a notoriously poor or confrontational relationship with the employee in question and if there's a very real possibility he or she will respond, "No, I'm not willing to have a conversation with you." In this case, you want to turn your invite into a statement such as, "We need to have a conversation about [insert issue here]." But be very careful here. You should forgo the invitation format only when a negative relationship exists. Otherwise, you risk damaging a neutral or positive relationship.

Disarm Yourself

No one wants to be on the receiving end of hurtful criticism. Most employees will let it slide from time to time if you lose your cool under stress and blow up a bit. However, if this form of criticism becomes a standard course of action for how you make corrections and instigate change, you're going to push employees, even Hundred Percenters, into reverse motion when it comes to tolerance and performance.

A hurtful criticism from the boss can trigger a chain reaction of work issues the employee might be silently holding inside. This can inspire a thought process that goes something like the following: "Fine. I know it's partly my fault that we lost the client. But did [insert boss's name] have to humiliate me like that? I'm the only one who pulls my weight around here. I'm stuck working with a bunch of slackers, and the one time I mess up, I get treated like this. I'm getting my résumé out there—today!"

If employees suspect that hurtful criticism is going to be part of the experience, they're likely to enter a constructive feedback conversation with some trepidation. This can prevent the important message from being heard. 100% Leaders avoid this situation by making a gesture that says, "No weapons of communication will be used against you in this conversation." This act of openly disarming themselves keeps talented employees feeling safe and open to the critical feedback being delivered.

Christian is a department manager with 25 direct reports. They're a good team, and he tries to be a fair boss, but pressure from his own superiors often results in Christian becoming hot-headed and emotional. When word got out that some members of Christian's team were using company time and computers to send e-mails and conduct other personal business, Christian's boss gave him an ultimatum to either change the behavior or change jobs.

Christian went back to his department and called an emergency meeting. As the members of his team filed into the conference room, they noticed Christian's face was beet red. His mouth was turned down in an ugly scowl, and his arms were crossed against his chest. "Here it comes again," they all anxiously thought. "Another verbal beating from Christian."

And they were right. Christian launched into his attack by basically repeating the Intimidator approach his own boss had used: "We're either gonna make some changes in attitude around here, or we're gonna make some changes in staff." His employees' walls of defensiveness shot up in every direction and blocked out everything else Christian had to say. And the Blame, Excuses, Denial, and Anxiety came out in full force.

The situation would have played out differently if Christian had taken a 100% Leader approach to delivering the constructive feedback. He could have (after taking adequate time out to cool off after being dressed down by his own boss) started the conversation by openly disarming himself in front of his employees. Then he could have tried approaching individuals or small groups personally and saying, "There have been some complaints about employees using the Internet for personal use during work hours. Would you be willing to meet with me to figure out how we can solve this problem? I want everyone to work together to find a comfortable resolution, so I'd like you to bring along any ideas you may have."

In this scenario, Christian disarmed himself by enforcing the fact that this would be a reciprocal conversation. His employees, who are used to his one-sided and hurtful criticisms (and who likely resent this behavior a great deal), would certainly take note of the change in his approach. And because Christian personally delivered the invitation in a calm and rational manner, he went the extra mile to show that this wouldn't be another anger session filled with blame and accusations.

Judgment is another verbal weapon that can shut down two-way communication and stand in the way of an effective employee critique. Openly expressing judgment quickly turns a conversation from constructive to destructive and will make employees feel incompetent and discouraged. Disarming yourself of judgment can be done by pausing midconversation and saying something like, "I'd like to review the situation to make sure I'm on the same page as you."

If you discover you're on a different wavelength than the employee, you'll need to backtrack and correct the situation. Taking this extra step doesn't mean you're going to necessarily agree with the other party, but it does send a reassuring message that you want to nonjudgmentally understand a perspective other than your own.

Eliminate Blame

The goal in delivering constructive feedback is not to make employees feel bad for whatever they may have done or thought. As I said earlier, most folks likely already know that they did something wrong, and chances are they're already suffering for it. Instead of assigning blame, 100% Leaders avoid historical and emotional punishment and focus on solutions. You may not share the same perspectives on situations as your employees do, but you can still work together to develop a plan that moves in a positive direction.

Because of historical evidence, Christian, our leader from the earlier example, has some work to do in order to show his employees that he has no further intention of playing the blame game. One way he can do this is to say in his invite to partner something like, "Look, if we find we have different perspectives, we can discuss them and develop a plan for moving forward." Or, if he finds himself in the middle of a conversation with an employee and he sees that a difference of opinion exists, he can acknowledge it by saying, "I see we have very different opinions on this. That's fine. But let's work together to find a resolution."

Affirm Their Control

In order to keep people fully engaged in a conversation that involves constructive feedback, it's important to reaffirm that they have some control over the situation. 100% Leaders do this by regularly asking, "Does that sound okay?" as the conversation progresses.

This simple question reminds employees that they have a say in the matter and that you care about how they're doing and what they're thinking. In Christian's case, this tactic would resolve much of the Denial, Blame, Excuses, and Anxiety his people are probably feeling. It would show that Christian is listening and that he cares, reaffirming the sincerity of his invite to partner in dialogue.

As an added bonus, affirming the other party's control is a quick check of whether that person remains receptive to your words. If the answer is, "No, that doesn't sound okay to me," or if you get a rapid-fire list of defensive questions in response, you can be pretty sure the conversation is off track. Again, you need to backtrack and fix this situation before you move on.

List Corrective Feedback

100% Leaders take nothing for granted when delivering constructive feedback. It's not that they doubt their employees' intelligence or feel the need to hypermanage. They simply recognize that it doesn't hurt to take the extra effort to make a crystal-clear statement that details exact expectations.

The golden rules for giving constructive feedback are that the feedback:

- Is specific
- Holds up to logical scrutiny
- Is understandable
- Teaches sufficiently

The following two techniques will ensure you cover every one of these golden rules.

Don't Skimp on the Details

No matter how small a detail may be, if it's something employees are going to be held accountable for, make sure you give them the information they need. This is especially important when delivering HARD Goals. A lot of leaders worry that giving minutely detailed constructive feedback makes them come off as control freaks or micromanagers. So they take conscious steps to temper their words and refrain from harping on the small details of how they want something done. But this often leaves employees without the direction they need.

No one wants to work under a micromanager. Certainly employees who feel they have the trust and confidence of the boss tend to remain more happily engaged in their work. But when clarity is sacrificed as part of the feedback, no one wins.

This simple principle establishes the dividing line between what constitutes micromanagement and constructive feedback: if something is not optional and if you will hold the employees accountable if they don't do it, you must give clear and logical feedback.

Nothing kills employee morale faster than when the boss withholds critical information and then admonishes employees when results fail to meet expectations. This happens in countless cases where the boss doesn't even realize he or she has failed to provide clear directions. Protect yourself and your employees from this situation by never assuming there is a thorough understanding of anything for which employees can be punished or fired.

Explain Why

One critical aspect of giving constructive feedback that most leaders miss is letting employees know *why* they're being asked to do something. This is often the factor that makes or breaks what employees do, how well they do it, and how happy they are doing it.

It is critical to note that if you abuse the power of why, you risk losing the effectiveness behind the why. If you really don't have a good reason for why you want something done a certain way, don't make the correction. Let some things be negotiable. Then, when a situation comes up where you really can't offer a why, whether due to confidentiality, the pressure of time, or some arbitrary rule from on high, you'll still have the trust and cooperation of your best people.

It's always a good idea to follow up constructive feedback in writing, including the why. Few of us have total recall, and some important detail is almost guaranteed to get lost. Putting it in writing also provides a visual aid, and that's important in today's world of seemingly endless auditory, visual, and sensory stimulation. Finally, when you've got it in writing, there can be no disputing what was said.

Synchronize Your Understanding

This final step is where the partnership aspect of the dialogue kicks in. Granted, if you're forced to correct an employee error, you likely already know the outcome you want. Usually it's for the employee to replace the undesirable behavior with a Hundred Percenter behavior. But you'll never win an employee's buy-in to change if you tell the employee to just shut up and follow orders.

When you say to an employee, "Tell me how you think we can work together to build on this and make things more effective next time," there's no overbearing rank being pulled. There's also no recrimination for the behavior you've called into question. It's just an invite to work together to make things better.

And because "Tell me how you think we can work together to build on this and make things more effective next time" is an open-ended question with no presumed answer, it encourages open discussion. On the contrary, asking, "Do you understand my feedback?" is closed off and makes you sound condescending, which will only raise the other person's defensiveness. Open-ended questions encourage communication that serves as a litmus test of how well your people understand your feedback.

Putting It All Together

To sum up the IDEALS technique, here's a quick review of the strategies and a simple script for each:

I   Invite them to partner: "Would you be willing to have a conversation with me about X, Y, Z? Does right now work, or would you rather wait until after lunch?"

D   Disarm yourself: "I'd like to review the situation to make sure I'm on the same page as you."

E   Eliminate blame: "If we have different perspectives, we can discuss those and develop a plan for moving forward."

A Affirm their control: "Does that sound okay to you?"

L List corrective feedback: "The behavior I am seeing is X, Y, Z, and what I need to see is A, B, C."

S Synchronize your understanding: "Tell me how you think we can work together to build on this and make things more effective next time."

Imagine the following situation: You put Joe, a good employee but not yet a Hundred Percenter, in charge of finalizing the itinerary for an important client meeting. Despite the fact that you've already seen several drafts of the itinerary, Joe shows up to today's client meeting empty-handed.

This leaves you looking unprepared and amateurish in front of the client. You're angry, but you pull through the meeting. Afterward you approach Joe to discuss what happened. Below are two options for starting your conversation.

Version A. "I gotta tell you, Joe, I'm pretty ticked about not having the itinerary. You obviously didn't listen when I said you were in charge of getting it done. Your irresponsibility made me look like a total fool. If you want to sabotage your career, that's fine, but don't screw up my career, too. If you're not going to do something, just tell me so I can do it myself like everything else."

Version B. "Joe, would you be willing to have a conversation with me about the missing itinerary? I'd like to review the situation to make sure I'm on the same page as you. And if we have a different perspective, which is totally possible, we'll work that out and come up with a plan for the future. Does that sound okay? Great. Do you have time now, or do you want to wait until after lunch?"

Which version is likely to make Joe receptive to the message you need to deliver about his performance? And which version is sending Joe the message that he's under attack and that he needs to raise his guard? The situation isn't going to get remedied until Joe changes his behavior, and you need his willing participation to make that happen.

It's clear that Version B is the 100% Leader choice. Here's one common complaint that some leaders have about Version B: "But I'm really ticked at Joe, and he needs to know that. He let me down, and I feel betrayed. Version B makes it sound like I'm letting Joe's behavior slide, and I can't allow that."

That's a legitimate response. We've all had those same thoughts, and we've all felt that same emotional itch wanting to be scratched. But here's the problem: despite what happened today, Joe is a talented employee, and we want to hold onto him while we help him improve his behavior and help him improve his performance. The question is whether making Joe defensive is the best way to accomplish that.

Version A is virtually guaranteed to make Joe defensive. If his defensiveness makes him aggressive, you're going to have a fight on your hands. If he becomes passive, he'll endure your emotional browbeating, but he may subtly sabotage you down the road.

Tweaking the IDEALS Script

I began this chapter by outlining the Stages of Accountability (Denial, Blame, Excuses, Anxiety, and Accountability). I then took you through the IDEALS script, designed to deliver critical feedback no matter what Stage of Accountability an employee is in. Now I'm going to offer one more tweak that combines the Stages of Accountability and the IDEALS script.

For many leaders, the $64,000 question is, "What do I actually say when I hear Denial, Blame, Excuses, and Anxiety, especially right before or after I've delivered the IDEALS script?" We designed the IDEALS script to work in every one of these Stages of Accountability. But you may do a little tweaking in how you deliver or repeat the IDEALS script depending on which stage the employee currently inhabits.

Denial

Denial may be the most frustrating stage a leader can face. When confronted with an employee who just doesn't "get it," there's a natural tendency to want to reach across the desk and throttle that person. Another similarly ineffective reaction is to soften the feedback. This typically involves throwing compliments in with the correction to try to make folks feel less defensive. It's called the Compliment Sandwich, and it's perhaps the worst management technique ever created. (We'll address this technique in depth in Chapter 3, "Reclaim Our Heroes with Positive Reinforcement.")

When confronted with Denial, you want to remain candid, but in a very calm and matter-of-fact way. You can't punch your way through a wall of defensiveness. Yelling and screaming just doesn't work. Hyperbole (i.e., exaggerating or "amping up" the seriousness of the issue at hand) is just as ineffective. Stick to the facts. Keep the conversation as specific, calm, and data-driven as you can. If you've completed the IDEALS script but the employee is still in Denial, go back and do it again with special emphasis on L: List corrective feedback.

Blame

When you give corrective feedback to someone in the Blame stage, you're likely to hear a reaction such as, "Well, I guess I could fix my part in this, but nothing's going to work until we fix Accounting." The party that gets blamed will typically be one outside your control, making such a reaction an attempt to deflate or completely deter any corrective action you intended to take.

The first time this happens is the signal that you need to actively redirect the focus of your conversation. Simply say, "All I want to focus on right now is what we can control." The Blamer will likely retort, "But Accounting is the real problem here," to which you can reply, "Accounting is not my concern. I want to discuss those issues that are under our control, right here, right now." Just as when folks are in the Denial stage, you may have to calmly and coolly repeat yourself a few times before your words are heard. Remember, there can be no conversation about blaming Accounting if you absolutely refuse to entertain the conversation.

Excuses

When you hear lots of excuses from your employees, it means they're under the impression that you're blaming them or about to blame them. (You may not actually be doing any blaming, but that's what they've internalized.) The simple response is to say, "I'm not interested in assigning any blame; I'm only interested in fixing the problem." Does this mean you excuse the behavior? Of course not. You're still going to track mistakes and failures, and this may result in poor reviews, action plans, and even dismissal. But the moment you hear an excuse, your primary concern has to be on fixing the issue. If you've got a project on deadline that needs to get out the door ASAP, you can do your employee write-up 15 minutes later. It's far more critical to act immediately to fix the problem and deliver the project.

Anxiety

When you hear Anxiety, you've got a person who is on the verge of Accountability. The employee understands his or her culpability and even understands the solution, but that person is overwhelmed by what comes next. In these cases, take your corrective feedback and break it into bite-sized chunks.

People in Anxiety mode need process steps (Step 1, we do this; Step 2, we do this; and so forth). Does it take a few extra minutes? Sure, but what are your options? If you let people wallow in their anxious state, they're not going to take care of the problem or change the behavior. So take your corrective feedback, break it up, and get them started. Plan for frequent check-ins and touch base with the employee after the first step to make any necessary corrections, then after the second step, and on down the line. Usually after the first two steps, Anxiety has diminished, and the employee is closer to, or already at, full Accountability.

Employees need corrective feedback to grow and get better on the job, and most employees actually want corrective feedback. The IDEALS script is a way to ensure employees don't spend their emotional energy denying, blaming, excusing, or being anxious about that feedback. The IDEALS script, with the adaptations mentioned above, will lower people's walls of defensiveness so they absorb your feedback, are accountable to that feedback, and use the feedback to become Hundred Percenters.

The Special Case of Talented Terrors

So far this chapter has been about using the IDEALS script to move good employees past the stages of Denial, Blame, Excuses, and Anxiety until they embrace Accountability. I want to finish the chapter by discussing "Talented Terrors," a specific kind of low-performing employee with the skills you want but with the attitude you don't want.

Most leaders admit that managing an employee with a bad attitude is difficult, but they stop short when it comes to labeling Talented Terrors as low performers: "You mean Jim in Accounting? I'll admit that he doesn't do anything without an argument first. But that's just who he is. Besides, he's got talent. He may have a lousy attitude, but he's still got what it takes to be a high performer."

Some people may believe Jim is a high performer, but 100% Leaders strongly disagree. They know that no matter how skilled an employee may be, if a bad attitude is part of the package, that person is not a Hundred Percenter, and there are no exceptions to the rule. HARD Goals and job successes aren't achieved by Hundred Percenter skill alone. They also require a Hundred Percenter attitude.

The critical mistake most leaders make in attempting to manage a bad attitude is taking a therapeutic approach. Given the day-to-day demands of the workplace, most leaders, even if they have the clinical training to do so, don't have the time and energy to take on the job of restructuring an employee's personality. Quite honestly, that's a job many qualified psychologists are even reluctant to tackle. But that doesn't mean the situation is hopeless. In many cases, you can't fix the underlying personality that drives a bad attitude, but you can put a stop to the behavioral manifestations of the bad attitude.

There are six rules for managing the behaviors that accompany a bad attitude:

1. Timeliness
2. Objectivity
3. Specificity
4. Candor
5. Calm
6. Choice

First we'll explore each rule on its own to see how it works. Then I'll show you how to combine all six rules into a simple script that can be used to defuse even the most undesirable behaviors.

Timeliness

Confront issues with Talented Terrors as they happen. Putting off until tomorrow what should be fixed today is one of the major flaws of yearly employee reviews. Besides, how many times of doing something wrong does it take to make it significant? If the Navy SEALs are launching a mission at 0600 hours and Chuck lumbers in at 0615 and says, "Sorry, but I had a late night," what do you think is going to happen? If a surgeon forgets to perform a critical procedure because she is in a rush to make a lunch date, is it excusable if only one patient is killed? Your circumstances might not be quite as life or death as these examples, but you don't have to let a series of bad situations pile up before you do something about a Talented Terror.

Deliver feedback about a bad attitude in real time, no more than 48 hours after the incident. This ensures that the facts are fresh and that you won't be approaching the conversation from a dangerous place of accumulated anger.

Objectivity

Talented Terrors are like anyone else when it comes to receiving bad news; they would rather not hear it. If they hear negative words such as *angry, disgusted, annoyed, unsupported, deceived, abused, controlled, punished, wronged, tricked,* or *used,* chances are good that they are going to check out of the conversation before it even gets started. And even if they do stay engaged, if you say something like, "I feel angry about your bad attitude," it only sends a subjective message about how you feel. The point here isn't about how you feel; it's about the employee's bad attitude manifested in bad behavior and why it needs to change.

Equally ineffective is a statement such as this: "If you got your work done on time, we'd achieve this HARD Goal and make my life a lot easier." This doesn't provide any objective facts that give the Talented Terror a reason to tune in to what you are saying. More than likely it will only inspire more negative thoughts such as, "Who cares how you feel or what I can do for you? I've got more important things to do on company time, like posting to my blog and downloading music from iTunes."

However, if you keep the statement objective and say, "Company policy states your responsibility is to fulfill your work commitments on time. I just went into a meeting with Client X without the information I needed because I didn't have your work," you're putting the unemotional and objective facts on the table. That presents a level of culpability that, even for the most calculating of Talented Terrors, is hard to evade.

Remaining objective during a conversation about bad attitude presents a challenge that many leaders don't know how to meet. That's because there's a common and incorrect belief that objectivity is dependent upon being able to make a quantifiable analysis of a situation. In other words, you need to be able to measure it.

But just because you can't assign a number to an attitude doesn't make the attitude invalid. In fact, it's easy to lay an objective claim on the outward expression of attitude: behavior. A bad attitude nearly always leaks out in the form of bad behavior, and behavior absolutely can be verified and observed.

Specificity

When tackling tough issues like attitude, it's critical to keep the conversation limited to specific events. Observable details about the bad behavior in question are what you're after, and you want those specifics at your fingertips. There's no need to inflate the specifics. If you've seen unacceptable behavior, you're allowed—and obligated—to address it, just as it is.

Being specific also means avoiding absolutes in the form of words like *always* and *never*. (Here's my rule: It is always a good idea to never use words like *always* and *never*.) Absolutes are hyperbole and only draw the emphasis away from the specifics. This can kill your chances of keeping the focus on the facts. No one is always or never anything. Are you always on time or never wrong? Probably not, and neither are your Talented Terrors.

Accusing a Talented Terror of always showing up late and never being productive in meetings is laying the groundwork for failed communication. The employee is only going to shrug off your accusation by dredging up the memory of some meeting that took place three years ago to which he or she not only arrived early but also brought the doughnuts. Remember, these folks have been honing their bad-attitude skills for a long time. They're good at it, and they're smart, which means you have to be smarter.

Candor

There can be no dodging the truth when you're talking to a Talented Terror about a bad attitude. It may seem kinder to surround a tough message in an attractive wrapper, but that won't get the facts out on the table, and it won't help to solve the problem. Fudging or inflating the truth doesn't do anyone any favors. You can't control how someone is going to react to your message, but you can control the message.

As I noted earlier, in Chapter 3 we'll fully take on the topic of the Compliment Sandwich, a common mistake managers make of trying to squeeze a negative performance critique or correction between layers of positive reinforcement. It doesn't work, and here's an example of why it doesn't work.

Imagine you're Frank, and your boss has just called you in for a little feedback: "Frank, you're a world-class programmer—the absolute best. You're probably the smartest guy in the department. You've been pretty nasty during our weekly meetings, and it's causing some hurt feelings. But I'm saying all this because you're just so darn talented, I want to see you really flourish."

What did you hear? If I'm Frank, I just heard: "You're great; you're smart." Blah blah blah blah. "You're great; you're smart."

Frank heard some compliments, then the "whaa-whaa-whaa" trombone effect of Charlie Brown's teacher, then some more compliments. But he certainly didn't hear anything about his job being in jeopardy or even his performance being anything other than great.

Not only is this message completely disingenuous, but no one remembers what happens in the middle. If you're really afraid that blatant candor will shut down the conversation, you can always use a softening statement—one that won't mask your message. Try saying something like, "Frank, I've got a tough message to deliver. There's no getting around it, but I want you to understand that I'm doing this out of a concern for your well-being; if you don't fix this stuff, your career here is in jeopardy." This softens the blow while enforcing the message: "Frank, you really need to listen to this."

Calm

Staying calm may sound trivial or obvious, but Talented Terrors have a unique ability to get under a leader's skin. Chances are that when you call these folks in to discuss a bad attitude, you're going to have some emotion behind it, usually some form of anger or frustration. However, if you lose your cool, your argument is going to come off as over-the-top and so lose impact.

Talented Terrors have had lots of time to hone their bad behavior. They're used to getting called on their bad attitude, and they're just waiting for you to get angry and speak without thinking. Because as soon as you say or do something illogical, they'll turn the situation around on you. And before you know it, you'll end up apologizing to them for *your* bad behavior.

The HALT approach is one that most 100% Leaders abide by. It's an easy and effective method of keeping anger and other unproductive emotions at bay. If you're hungry, angry, lonely, or tired (HALT), all of which are emotionally compromised positions, delay the conversation until your mood shifts or you can get some sleep or food. It's not like you're trying to step out on the discussion or avoid it; you're just rescheduling it.

Choice

Leadership grants you a certain level of authority, but you still can't force people to do something against their wills. If you try to back Talented Terrors into a corner, their behavior will just get worse. They'll also become defensive and assume an attacking position that makes it even harder to reach the resolution you want. This is the complete opposite of what you want to achieve; your goal is to eradicate the behaviors associated with Talented Terrors.

All you can do is outline the choices and enforce the consequences. At that point, it's up to your Talented Terrors to decide to walk away, continue with their bad behavior and face the outlined negative consequences, or change their behavior and enjoy the reward of positive consequences. But while the choice is up to them, you can still control how long they have to make that choice.

After you lay out the facts and outline the consequences, offer your Talented Terrors the option of taking 24 hours to think things over. You've likely given them a lot to take in, and they alone bear the burden of making a decision about how they will respond. With some time to think it over, they're going to make a smarter decision—one they are more likely to abide by.

Script for Tying Together the Six Rules

By following the six rules, it's easy to construct a script that will address any attitude issue. Let's take a look at how it all comes together:

> Joe, I've called you in today because there's a problem with your recent performance. In Tuesday's task force meeting you made three biting and sarcastic remarks during our brainstorming session, and that's just not acceptable behavior for that setting. This will not be allowed to continue.
>
> Now, I can't force you to change, and I won't try. So you have a choice: you can change your behavior or keep it where it is. If you change, you will be much more effective, and I think you'll see your teammates respond more positively. If you decide to change, I can work with you to outline a very specific action plan with clear expectations. If you opt not to change, then we'll begin an improvement plan which, without significant progress, could ultimately result in termination. [Insert your own HR policies here.]
>
> Joe, I believe you are capable of changing this behavior. But only you can choose the path that's right for you. Just be clear that there are only two options here, and maintaining your present course is not one of them. You can give me your decision right now, or you can take 24 hours to make a decision.

How to Deal with the Response

After you deliver the script, there are a number of responses you might get. A perfect response would be acceptance. For instance, Joe would say, "You're absolutely correct, and I want to get back on track right away."

Typically, when you deliver the script correctly, it will go one of two ways. You're going to get either acceptance or the complete opposite, where the employee states an unwillingness to play by the rules and expresses a desire to just get out.

But sometimes you'll get a slightly different response such as:

Denial. "But I didn't do anything wrong."

Narcissism. "You can't come down on me; I'm the best person you've got!"

Anger. "How dare you insult me like this."

Blame. "Bob's the one you should be talking to; he's the one who always messes up."

Drama. This includes tears or other forms of histrionics.

Regardless of the response you get, there's a simple technique that keeps the conversation on track. It's what psychologists call the broken record technique, and it works just the way it sounds: "I hear you; now let me repeat [insert script here]." And you walk the employee through the whole script again.

The broken record technique works as long as you stick to the script and don't indulge whatever defense the Talented Terror is offering up. These folks may be low performers, but they're not stupid. As I've said, they are often brilliant, and they are much better at having a bad attitude than you are at managing it. The only chance you have at keeping the communication on track and not allowing yourself to be manipulated is to stick to the script and the six rules. You might have to repeat the script two or three times, but after that it's time to say, "Okay, I have made my point. This conversation is over."

Sticking to the script and keeping the conversation on track can feel a bit awkward at first. And Talented Terrors will try every trick they know to get you off your script. Keep in mind that good leadership is by and large a performing art. As with any performer, you need to practice. If you have teenagers, they typically love to play the role of Talented Terror, and they make wonderful practice partners. They'll give you every form of bad attitude and drama you can think of, and that will force you to get comfortable with calmly repeating yourself.

Conclusion

We started the chapter by talking about the Stages of Accountability, a five-stage psychological journey that starts at Denial and moves through Blame, Excuses, and Anxiety before reaching Accountability. The six-step IDEALS script opens up a dialogue that helps employees to move past these other stages so they can reach Accountability:

Step 1. Invite them to partner.
Step 2. Disarm yourself.
Step 3. Eliminate blame.
Step 4. Affirm their choices.
Step 5. List corrective feedback.
Step 6. Synchronize your understanding.

Talented Terrors are the low-performing employees with the skills you want but the bad attitudes you don't want. Attitude manifests in behavior. The six rules of Timeliness, Objectivity, Specificity, Candor, Calm, and Choice allow you to effectively manage Talented Terrors so that they discontinue the behaviors that accompany their bad attitudes.

3

Reclaim Our Heroes with Positive Reinforcement

Leadership IQ's Hundred Percenter Index Questions

My leader distinguishes between high and low performers.

My leader recognizes my accomplishments with praise.

This organization shares its success stories with its employees.

Introduction

Here's a shocking finding: when we asked more than 5,000 employees to tell us who teaches them more about dos and don'ts on the job—the boss or their fellow employees—67% said they learn more by watching fellow employees.

This should make you wonder what your employees learn about being a Hundred Percenter from watching their coworkers. Let me offer two very bad lessons that the typical employee is learning every single day.

Lesson #1: Being a Hundred Percenter Stinks

Imagine it's Friday afternoon at 4 p.m. and you've got a major report due on Monday at 9 a.m. This report could derail your career if it's not done right, and you're going to need some help getting it finished. It's going to be a tough weekend of hard work, but a deadline is a deadline. Who are you going to turn to for help: the employee who gives 100% effort or the employee who gives 50% effort? Of course, you take the Hundred Percenter. When the same situation arises again next week, who do you think gets called on to make the painful sacrifice? The Hundred Percenter. And it's the Hundred Percenter who will get the call the weekend after that and the weekend after that.

Now answer this question: Who has the worst job in your department? Say it with me: the Hundred Percenter. There are two lessons here: First, you need to create more Hundred Percenters (just follow all the rules in this book). Second, when your non–Hundred Percenters are looking at your Hundred Percenters, they're probably not learning the lesson that you hope they are. Instead, they're likely learning that being a Hundred Percenter is hard and painful, a lesson that results in their saying, "No thank you" to that job!

Lesson #2: The Boss Can't Tell the Difference Between Hundred Percenters and Fifty Percenters

Imagine you've got two employees who just finished meeting a deadline for a tough project. Chris, a Hundred Percenter, did an incredible job (while giving 100% effort). Pat, a Fifty Percenter, did a passable job (no glaring mistakes, just not nearly as good a job as the Hundred Percenter). Now they're both standing in front of you waiting for some feedback. Here's what the typical manager says: "Chris and Pat, thanks for getting this done on time, good work."

What did they learn? Pat learned that giving 50% and doing passable work is totally fine. Pat's thinking, "Heck, giving 100% must be for chumps if we both just got the same feedback." Chris learned that giving 100% doesn't get noticed, and Chris is thinking, "How many more times am I going to give 100% when the boss seems to think that 50% is every bit as good as 100%?"

Why Are We Teaching These Terrible Lessons?

It's easy to dump everything on Hundred Percenters. And in the short term, developing more Hundred Percenters to spread the load takes more work than just abusing the few we've already got. Yes, the bill will come due when those Hundred Percenters quit, but as we've seen in other chapters, for many folks, denial ain't just a river in Egypt.

We also do a lousy job of distinguishing between Hundred Percenters and everyone else. It's easy to let our compensation systems differentiate Hundred Percenters (assuming your compensation systems actually do that). But it's a lot harder to differentiate Hundred Percenters when a whole department is standing there, waiting to hear what you say. We hesitate to spotlight individuals, even with praise, often due to early training from parents and teachers who warned, "Don't make Pat feel bad" or "Don't play favorites" or "Doing well is its own reward."

We're not allowed to play favorites on the basis of race, age, religion, gender, sexual preference, health status, and all the rest—

and that's a good thing. But we *are* allowed to play favorites on the basis of performance (or effort or teamwork or grit or anything controllable and job related). If I'm Phil Jackson coaching the 1996 Chicago Bulls, I'm allowed to have a favorite player (Michael Jordan). I'm allowed to have a second favorite player (Scottie Pippen). I'm even allowed to have third favorite players (anybody who gets those two guys the ball). There's no law that says I have to give equal praise to people who don't play their positions or who miss their shots.

Not only are leaders allowed to differentiate Hundred Percenters, but if they want to be successful, they're required to do so. Across our employee survey database, comprising hundreds of thousands of employee survey respondents, over 70% of people say that Hundred Percenters should receive more rewards and recognition than others.

The challenge is twofold: we've got to keep our Hundred Percenters continually striving to give 100%, and we've got to teach everyone else how and why to become a Hundred Percenter. In the sections that follow, I'll show you how to recognize your Hundred Percenters and keep them motivated—without throwing money at them. Second, I'll show you how to use a related technique to teach and motivate everyone else to become a Hundred Percenter.

Ending Our Reliance on Money

"I'd love to have even one Hundred Percenter," said Joe, who heads the claims processing department of an insurance company. "I'm in charge of 30 people, and while the work isn't brain surgery, it is target oriented." Joe estimates his team is primarily made of Fifty to Seventy-Five Percenters, satisficers. "They get the work done okay,"

Joe says, "but we're rarely on schedule, and that affects a lot of people. Some days I feel like the most hated guy on the planet."

When Joe was asked how he motivates his team, his frustration showed: "My hands are tied when it comes to financial incentives. The company does a yearly review along with standard percentage raises. So nobody's getting stoked over that. I do what I can, birthdays with the cake and balloons, anything to inspire a sense of team. Look, we push paper around in my department. It's far from exciting. Without money, there's no real motivation for anyone to do anything."

Joe, like a lot of people, believes money inspires people to give their best efforts. However, if you ask your Hundred Percenters what drives them to deliver high performance, most will list a lot of things before they even get to money. Hundred Percenters need and appreciate money, but more than that, they're after the feel-good emotional charge that comes from working hard at a job that makes a difference in the world.

"Oh, you're talking about praise," Joe responds. "I know all about praise, and it's not for me. This is work, not Disneyland. If people want to get warm fuzzies just for showing up every day, they're in the wrong place."

Once again, Joe is making a common mistake—one that keeps a lot of would-be Hundred Percenters firmly rooted in satisficing. It's easy to understand why so many leaders make this error. The blame lies with what has largely been the mantra of our times: "Praise early, praise often." Joe's right; the world, and especially our country, got too soft, things got too easy, and a lot of people got put on a pedestal for doing absolutely nothing special.

But there's a shift going on in the world—and in this country. There is a cry for change, and it applies to our government, our homes, and our workplaces. It's time to reclaim a culture that honors a genuine work ethic and to push ourselves to greatness again. But we still need to commend the folks who go above and beyond—if we want them to keep giving Hundred Percenter effort.

Positive Reinforcement Instead of Praise

Positive reinforcement isn't praise. It's a teaching tool that addresses a well-documented psychological principle that says that desirable behavior—when reinforced—gets repeated. Leaders who communicate a clear message that says "The thing you just did right there was good; do more of it" deliver positive feedback that increases the frequency and intensity of Hundred Percenter behavior. These are the leaders who keep their Hundred Percenters on track with high performance and who make non–Hundred Percenters eager to go above and beyond.

One of our studies found that bosses who give significant positive recognition to Hundred Percenters get 270% more buy-in when they assign HARD Goals. And yet 61% of employees say their boss does a lousy job of recognizing and acknowledging their accomplishments. Take Marilynne, for instance, who works in retail and who went out of her way to help a customer obtain the out-of-stock items he needed. When the customer wrote a letter to the store commending Marilynne's performance, her boss merely put the letter in with her paycheck. He never said a word about it.

When we asked leaders why they hold back from giving deserved positive reinforcement, the overwhelming response was "I don't do positive reinforcement, even with my top talent. It just feels too much like praise."

But then there are leaders like Frank, who do teach and inspire their people through positive reinforcement. When Adrienne, a paralegal at Frank's organization, noticed that some client files were missing important documents, she quickly brought it to Frank's attention. A survey of the organization's filing system revealed that the employee in charge of filing, who had recently been fired, had really messed up the task. Contracts for one client were in another client's file, and there was a huge fear that some contracts may have gone missing entirely.

Adrienne volunteered to overhaul the filing system, a job that would require extra hours and even some weekends. As she sorted through the mess, she recognized that even where things were filed correctly, the whole system was outdated and inefficient. She put together a proposal for an improved system. Frank loved her proposal and asked Adrienne to implement the new system with the help of a temp. It took two weeks of focused work, but finally every missing contract and document had been accounted for and correctly filed.

Frank recognized that Adrienne's commitment to seeing the job through, and her incentive to go above and beyond, was the kind of Hundred Percenter attitude he wanted on his team. In addition to thanking Adrienne, Frank threw a department lunch in her honor. Frank also called Adrienne into his office to discuss her future with the company, including some special projects she might want to be part of. These positive gestures of recognition, none of which involved extra compensation, gave Adrienne a boost that made her feel even more engaged on the job.

Most leaders wait until employees do something wrong and then give negative feedback. Negative reinforcement can work to cease unwanted behavior, but as anyone who has been on the receiving end of negative reinforcement knows, the common response is to figure out the best way to avoid getting "yelled at" again. Negative reinforcement might stop the employee behavior you don't want, but there's no guarantee that the behavior that replaces it will be even close to what you do want.

Positive reinforcement is a powerful teaching tool that tells employees the kind of performance you want to see again. Stop waiting for your employees to do something wrong and start noticing—and commenting—when they deliver exceptional performance.

The Four Components of Positive Reinforcement

There are four components you definitely want to hit when delivering positive feedback:

Make it meaningful.
Be specific.
Make it timely: catch 'em in the act.
Keep it free of criticism.

Let's take a closer look at how positive reinforcement works—and how you can make it work for you.

Make It Meaningful

You don't need to blow constant smoke to make and maintain Hundred Percenters. In fact, doling out meaningless praise is guaranteed to work against you. Say you tell your employee, Mary, who typically gives 100% effort, "Great job" whenever she truly deserves it. But then you also say "Great job" to Bob, who typically slides by with no more than 75% effort.

What Bob just heard is that by satisficing, he's just as good as Mary, which won't inspire Bob to work harder and become a Hundred Percenter. Mary, however, heard that her 100% is no better than Bob's satisficing. Mary's logical next thought is, "Why even bother giving 100% effort when 75% gets me the same reward?" Mary is ticked off, and her performance may slack because of it. She might even start to doubt her abilities and lose her Hundred Percenter edge. Don't worry about Bob, though. Right now Bob's feeling pretty good about his less than best effort.

Only low performers are happy when rewards are vague or distributed on a widespread level. Hundred Percenters want feedback that provides a learning curve and that differentiates their great performance from everyone else's.

One leader, Tom, found this out the hard way thanks to an employee who had the guts to speak out. Tom's company was executing a hard mailing that was being done in-house. He assigned Madison, one of his employees, to stuff envelopes. In the past, Madison had shown signs of being a Hundred Percenter, and Tom wanted to keep her engaged and moving toward that goal. So he called Madison into his office on the first day of the mailing project to deliver a little psychological boost.

"I'm really impressed with your efforts today," Tom said. "Your work on this mailing project is really terrific."

When all Madison did was to stare at him blankly, Tom asked her what was on her mind. "You're kidding, right?" Madison asked.

Tom replied, "No, I really want you to know what a great job you are doing."

Madison fidgeted for a few seconds and then said, "This is hard for me to say to my boss, but if I don't say it, I'll regret it. Look, I'm stuffing envelopes right now. I mean, I know the job has to get done, and I don't mind doing it, but really, anyone could do this job. What I'd really like is to know what you thought of my work on last month's ACME report. I worked really hard on that report, and I'd like to take on more projects like it, but I have no idea if my work is good or where it needs improvement."

Madison was brave. Most employees don't feel safe speaking this openly to the boss. But her words are true. Empty praise holds no value for Hundred Percenters or even potential Hundred Percenters. It just kills their desire to work harder and diminishes their trust in you as their leader.

Be Specific

Daniel, the director of a small community hospital, is always on the lookout for opportunities to compliment his team on their good work. Whenever he sees commendable performance, he tells employees, "Looking good" or "Keep up the great work." But despite his good intentions, Daniel's words are too vague to deliver any message of real value.

"Great job" doesn't qualify as positive reinforcement. It's empty praise that delivers a zero learning curve. In order to be effective, positive feedback must provide a clear picture of the specific performance that's being commended. Even tacking on "I like your attention to detail" doesn't specify what details about the behavior you actually liked and want to see again. If you want employees to repeat the performance, you've got to tell them exactly what they did right.

Once Daniel learned the importance of being specific, he stopped handing out vague compliments. Now he "paints" a clear verbal picture of the great work he wants to see replicated. For example, Daniel told one high-performing employee, "Aaron, the way you got Mr. X's tests done ahead of schedule means a lot to both me and Mr. X. And the new format you created to record the test results addresses all the breakdowns I asked for. Keep bringing me your great ideas for improvement."

Aaron walked away from this short meeting with a lot of helpful feedback. He's thinking, "You know, I did do a good job with

Mr. X. I had to give up my lunch and really hustle to get those lab results in on time, but it sure was worth it. I wasn't sure about the new format, but I guess it was a good idea. I wonder what else I can do to make things better around here."

Positive reinforcement should provide a clear visualization of the specific skills and abilities that constitute the high performance effort you're commending. Effective positive reinforcement keeps current Hundred Percenters firmly on track of what makes them the best and gives potential Hundred Percenters clear guidelines for how the organization measures Hundred Percenter performance. This gives employees the ability to self-assess their own performance, and to self-correct, in order to reach or surpass that same level of high performance again.

As an added benefit, other employees who witness the positive reinforcement, such as any employees who overheard Daniel commending Aaron, will also know what it takes to be a high performer. Positive reinforcement is effective and infectious.

Make It Timely: Catch 'Em in the Act

Positive reinforcement depends on a brain connection that associates the positive message with the desired action or behavior. That's not going to happen if too much time passes between when the good employee behavior occurs and when you deliver your feedback. Besides, asking employees (especially Hundred Percenters) to wait months for a yearly review to get some feedback is like asking them to wait an eternity. Most employees want performance feedback that's relevant to the work they're doing right now. In order for positive reinforcement to carry full impact, it has to be delivered in real time.

This doesn't mean wandering about the workplace offering meaningless praise. It does mean looking for teachable moments and giving supportive documentation as those moments happen. When Aaron, in the story above, had the test results done early, Daniel was right there to say, "Hey. You got this done ahead of schedule, and that's terrific." Think about the impact of that message 6, 8, or 12 months after the fact. If Daniel even remembered to include it in a yearly review, it would likely leave Aaron scratching his head and wondering, "What test results? I don't even remember a Mr. X."

Keep It Free of Criticism

There's a place and time for constructive feedback in the workplace, but it isn't when you're delivering a positive message. As I mentioned in Chapter 2, too many leaders make the mistake of trying to squeeze a negative performance critique or correction between layers of positive reinforcement. This is called the Compliment Sandwich, and it's a crazy mixed message that gets zero results.

Joanne wanted to motivate one of her employees, Ashley, to more closely follow company customer-service policy. Some things about Ashley's performance were outstanding, close to Hundred Percenter, and so Joanne didn't want to demotivate her with negative feedback. She decided to soften the criticism by lacing it in with a few compliments. That way she figured she could help Ashley correct her mistakes while still reinforcing her strengths that were a value to the company.

She pulled Ashley aside and said, "You did a great job dealing with that difficult customer last week. She was visibly upset, but you kept your cool and helped her resolve the problem. Satisfied customers are what we like to create. I did notice you arguing with another customer this afternoon though, and that isn't so good. But again, last week, you were right on target."

Ashley returned to the selling floor, and Joanne hoped that her goal to soften the criticism with positive reinforcement would result in Ashley's improvement. Ashley's coworkers were on her in an instant; curious about what had just gone down with Joanne. "Oh, it was nothing bad," Ashley told them. "Remember that crazy customer I had last week? I guess Joanne is happy I didn't flip out on her or anything. I don't know. I'm not really sure what Joanne wanted. I guess she was just trying to tell me I'm doing a good job."

Joanne struck out on both counts by using a Compliment Sandwich. Her positive message was received, but it was clouded by the negative feedback layered in the middle. As for the constructive criticism, it wasn't heard at all. If anything, Ashley got a slight boost that her performance was good, but the negative behavior remained untouched.

The problem with the Compliment Sandwich is that no one remembers what happens in the middle. Consider for a moment that you and two of your coworkers have each been given the opportunity to present a project before the board. Based upon the presentations, only one project will be chosen for funding. Are you going to want to speak first, second, or third? Most people opt for the third or first slot and do anything to avoid the dreaded middle position. Don't allow your message to become the ignored middle child. Get it out there in plain sight because if your message isn't being heard, you aren't doing anything to resolve the problem.

Positive reinforcement requires being in the moment with something that was done right. Don't waste the opportunity by trying to turn it into a buffer for bad news. If you have to deliver corrections or criticisms, keep it for another time. And make sure that when the employee responds to the criticism and delivers the desirable behavior, you let that employee know, right away and in detail, what he or she did right.

Performance Appraisals

Giving frequent positive feedback helps Hundred Percenters achieve their personal best. However, performance appraisals are another story. We conducted a study that showed only 14% of employees feel performance appraisals provide meaningful and relevant feedback.

Despite the fact that these reviews tend to produce minimal results, many organizations still enforce them. If you find yourself in a position where you have no choice but to comply, the following are some steps you can take to conduct a more effective performance appraisal. As a bonus, you may extract some valuable performance information.

Before you go into the review meeting, ask employees to give you a list of their proudest moments. This ensures that you recognize and reward any meritorious behavior that you might have missed or forgotten. A list of proudest moments also serves as an predictor for how the meeting will go. If an employee says "making it to work 80% of the time" was his proudest moment, you know you're in for a tougher time than with the employee who says, "I won the most prestigious award in my industry and got 27 of my studies published."

Putting It Together

Janice is the executive director of a senior living community. She loves both the organization and her job, and she generally commands the respect of her staff and is well liked. However, Janice worries that giving out positive reinforcement, which she associates with praise, will make her look like a pushover.

April, Parker, and Trent are three of Janice's employees, and all have Hundred Percenter potential. They're good at what they do, and they typically give their best efforts. However, all three share a similar feeling of disappointment that Janice rarely provides them with positive feedback. April recently confided in a few of her peers that she's looking for another job. She said she wants to work for an organization that recognizes her talent and appreciates her efforts.

Workplace grapevines being what they are, Janice soon learned that April, Parker, and Trent were unhappy—and why. Janice realized she was going to have to make some changes in her leadership style. She took it a step at a time. Trent was working on a calendar of resident outings, and despite working on the project for more than a week, the calendar remained empty. Janice had been considering turning the job over to Parker and had mentioned as much to Trent. She hoped the threat of losing a fun work assignment would act as negative reinforcement and give Trent some incentive to kick it into gear, but so far it hadn't worked.

She pulled Trent aside and asked him how the job was progressing. It was like someone let the air out of him. Trent's whole body physically deflated, and his energy just seemed to vanish. But his mind was racing with the following thoughts: Janice had already laid into him twice this week about the stupid calendar. He had dozens of calls out; it wasn't his fault that nobody was returning them. He was tired of talking about the calendar. Janice had nothing good to say to him. It was like she was out to get him.

Janice didn't know what Trent was thinking, but his silence and tense body language indicated to her that it wasn't anything good. She jumped right in with this rehearsed statement, "I was just looking at your call log, Trent. I'm impressed with the creative thought you've given to this project. We've never had a program coordinator who thought of outings like foreign films and classes at the meditation center. I also see you're trying to get us into the Degas exhibition at the museum next month. Our residents will really appreciate your hard work. They're always excited about new experiences."

Trent was pleasantly shocked to have Janice speak to him on this level. He actually was enjoying his work on the calendar. He was just frustrated that he couldn't get any results. For the first time he felt like he could trust Janice and ask her for help without risking getting yelled at. "Yeah, I'm pretty excited about those things too," Trent said. "I have a buddy who works at the museum who can even get us our own tour guide. I'm just not hearing back from anyone with a definite yes. What do you suggest I do?" Janice couldn't be happier. It was the first time Trent had asked for her advice. Together they explored some of the ways he could secure dates with his contacts, and he eagerly returned to his desk to get to work.

Later that day, Janice noticed April reviewing the monthly resident invoices. This was a sore spot around the residence, as invoices often contained mistakes and went out late. Janice had made it clear when she delegated this task to April that she wanted it done on time, and here April was doing as asked.

Janice jumped right on this opportunity to deliver some positive reinforcement. "April, I'm thrilled you're reviewing the invoices on schedule. You do a great job scheduling your work and meeting your deadlines. I feel a lot of confidence in your work, and the residents are going to be really happy to get these invoices on time and without error."

The genuine smile Janice got in response from April told her plenty. Lately it had seemed as if April was never happy on the job. She buried her head in her work and then scurried out at the end of the day. Her performance remained good, but her passion had definitely been lacking. Janice hoped that some positive reinforcement would effect a change in April's engagement level.

Since things were going so well, Janice decided to seek out Parker and try a little positive feedback on him. She found him creating a spreadsheet outlining the next week's work schedule. Too many of her staff had weak computer skills, and Parker's technical competence was a huge relief for Janice. "Parker, it's so nice to know I can rely on you to do the schedule," she said. "I really appreciate your ability with Excel."

Parker shot her a quizzical look, and Janice immediately recognized her error. To Parker, the Excel task was no more than rudimentary work that he was basically stuck with because no one else knew how to do it. She immediately said, "I'm sorry, I said the wrong thing. Excel is just one thing that gives you value around here. I really just wanted you to know that you're doing a good job."

As the words came out, Janice realized she'd blundered again. She'd offered no specific reference to what Parker did that made him so valuable. But then she noticed him smiling, and when he said, "Thanks, Janice. I really do appreciate it," she knew there was an opportunity for another chance. She'd wait for a genuine teachable moment and try again.

Creating Heroes with Storytelling and the Multiplier Technique

Giving employees one-on-one positive reinforcement is a great way to create and maintain Hundred Percenters. But there's also a way to sound a universal call that turns the drive to become a Hundred Percenter viral. It's a method that gets most members of your staff, from the new summer intern right on up to higher management, to start talking among themselves about the benefits of being a Hundred Percenter.

We call it the multiplier technique, and all it takes is a talent you probably, to some extent, already use every day: storytelling.

Except instead of talking about the big fish you caught up at the lake, or whatever amazing thing your five-year-old accomplished now, you're going to turn the folks who display Hundred Percenter effort into role models, or heroes. It's their stories of achievement you're going to tell. And because of the motivating force of these stories, your people are going to want to keep talking about the stories, creating a domino effect that gets your story—and the lesson it teaches—told time and time again.

Hundred Percenter Stories

Most of us tell stories every day, but Hundred Percenter storytelling is not about weaving the most scintillating yarn you can think of. It's got to be a story that's interesting enough to hold your listeners' attention, but more important, it has to inspire an emotional reaction that teaches a Hundred Percenter lesson. The way to deduce whether or not a story has what it takes to succeed is by looking at how the story ends—before you think about how it begins.

There's a great Hundred Percenter story that has become legendary among employees of the Ritz-Carlton, an organization renowned for inspiring Hundred Percenter effort. The story is good, but the ending is what drives the lesson home. As it's told, a family comes to stay at a Ritz-Carlton hotel in Bali. The family is traveling with a young child who suffers from food allergies that are so life threatening that the family has to bring special milk and eggs so the child can safely eat.

When the family arrives at the hotel, they find the food they are carrying has spoiled. A search is made of the island, and no proper food substitutes can be found. The family starts making hurried plans to return home when one of the hotel chefs remembers a market he had seen in Singapore. He is sure this market carries the items the boy needs, and upon placing a call, it's affirmed. He contacts his mother-in-law in Singapore, and she agrees to fly to Bali and deliver the food items. The Ritz-Carlton picks up the cost of the plane ticket, the boy gets his food, and the chef gets an unplanned visit from his mother-in-law.

The reason this story is so effective is because any employee who hears it also hears the lesson that "at the Ritz-Carlton, we go above and beyond." Granted, not everyone has family in Singapore, but the actions that employee took are repeatable behaviors that are desirable in the Ritz-Carlton culture where employees are trained under the motto "We are Ladies and Gentlemen serving Ladies and Gentlemen." This is the story of one gentleman doing for others.

The year 1997 marked the passing of two remarkable women, Diana, Princess of Wales, and Mother Teresa of Calcutta. They died within days of each other, and the media made much of their similarities. But the fact is, aside from the charitable activities they took part in, these two women could not have been more different.

Princess Diana may have been known as the People's Princess, but the fact remains that she was a princess, a title not many of us get to hold in our lifetimes. Typically, for a "commoner," the journey toward becoming a princess starts at birth. You're born into an elite crowd, you know the right people, you wear the right things, and you go to the right places. You know not everyone in your group is going to get the big prize, but you also know if you play your cards right, you've got a fighting chance of marrying a prince.

On the other hand, there's Mother Teresa. Unlike Diana, she was born into average circumstances. She wasn't pushed to greatness as part of her birthright. Rather, she made an independent choice to do something extraordinary with her life. This is not to dismiss or undercut the great things Diana accomplished during her lifetime. But when you look at which of these two women is the more viable hero for the "everyman"—which of their behaviors would be easier to duplicate—hands down, Mother Teresa wins.

Ironically, the media coverage of Princess Diana, her life, and her death, was 100 times greater than the media coverage given to Mother Teresa. But the media had a different intention in creating their multiplier effect. Even though both women accomplished amazing things, let's face it, it's a whole lot more glamorous to be a princess than a poor nun. Diana's story guaranteed better ratings. But what if the media's primary focus had been on Mother Teresa? Would that have more inspired the "common folk" to think about how they could give more of themselves to make the world a better place? It probably would have.

When you set out to create a Hundred Percenter story, look for a Mother Teresa story, one that anyone can replicate, and not an out-of-reach Princess Diana story. The time the garbage in the lunchroom caught fire, and Carl from marketing rushed in with a fire extinguisher and saved the day, is a great story. The problem is that it's a story about a once-in-a-lifetime event (we hope!). However, the time Carl worked through the weekend to fully implement a new brand for the company teaches a Hundred Percenter lesson other people can apply to their own day-to-day work. You'll know the stories that have the greatest teaching potential when their endings are in sync with the behaviors you need most from your people.

You'll find your Hundred Percenter stories right in your workplace. Just go out to your front lines and observe and talk to your people. Poke around for details that can be "sexed up" and made into engaging stories. Solicit your team, your managers, and your customers by asking, "Tell me about a time when you, another employee, or someone in this organization really knocked it out of the park." Then determine if anything you hear reinforces the specific Hundred Percenter behavior you want to see replicated. Make sure it's also got that great, emotion-driven, performance-lesson ending I mentioned above.

Don't just look to your proven Hundred Percenters for your stories. It's important to cast the storytelling spotlight evenly on both known high performers and surprise performers: satisficers who pulled off a Hundred Percenter move. This serves the dual purpose of keeping your current Hundred Percenters motivated and working at top form and inspiring your satisficers to reach for more. The goal is to turn as many folks as you can into heroes, as long as they deserve it.

Storytelling Follow-Up

Some Hundred Percenter stories will take off like wildfire, while others might need a little push to get going. Either way, you want to do your part to keep the story alive. I suggest two methods. The first is sparking a conversation with your people right after you tell the story. A question as simple as "What can each of us do to create a similar story?" will get the mental juices flowing. You might even get some information that leads to new stories, such as an employee who says, "Hey, remember that time the company mechanic was out sick and I fixed the delivery truck myself? That's sort of the same kind of story."

The other method is to incorporate these stories into daily or weekly meetings. The Ritz-Carlton conducts its famous daily line-ups, where every employee participates in a 15-minute meeting to discuss the obvious (like which king or prime minister is checking in that day), but also to review their Gold Standards and the stories that exemplify them.

Other clients conduct daily huddles or weekly reviews, where 10 minutes is devoted to highlighting one of these Hundred Percenter stories. The key is to tell the stories regularly (never assume people know them) so that you set a high bar for performance and teach people exactly what they need to do to clear that bar.

Conclusion

I began the chapter by identifying two of the bad lessons most employees are learning:

Lesson #1. Being a Hundred Percenter stinks.
Lesson #2. The boss can't tell the difference between Hundred Percenters and Fifty Percenters.

Employees learn from other employees, and given how we typically treat our Hundred Percenters, the lessons aren't great. But when we harness the power of positive reinforcement and use the multiplicative impact of viral stories to spread that positivity, we start to teach these very different lessons:

Lesson #1. Being a Hundred Percenter gets noticed.
Lesson #2. Being a Hundred Percenter gets rewarded.
Lesson #3. There are very specific and teachable steps to becoming a Hundred Percenter.

4

Shoves and Tugs

Leadership IQ's Hundred Percenter Index Questions

When I share my work problems with my leader, he/she responds constructively.

My leader removes the roadblocks to my success.

Introduction

100% Leaders are so successful at getting employees to meet and surpass hard challenges because they establish connections that inspire their people to aspire to greatness. 100% Leaders send a message that says, "I expect Hundred Percenter performance from you, but I also care about your success and fulfillment." However, 100% Leaders are never Appeasers (the kind of leaders who send the message, "You only have to do work you like; everything you are doing is terrific; I want to do whatever it takes to make you happy"). Appeasing isn't leading; it's placating. It will never make you feel genuinely good about your leadership skills, and it won't create a change in the status quo.

The first critical lesson of being a 100% Leader is: If the status quo felt bad, people would have changed already. If your people have been coasting by with moderate effort, decent results, and even minimal praise, where's the incentive to do anything differently? If you're going to change the status quo and ask for Hundred Percenter performance, you need to back it up with some solid evidence that being a Hundred Percenter is worth the extra effort.

Does Money Work?

The good news is that the motivators most Hundred Percenters value aren't tied to money. The same goes for the employees who will make the leap to Hundred Percenter performance. That's not to say money doesn't have a motivational impact, especially if your people are paid below market. But if you look at the reasons why people check out of their jobs, study after study shows money has little to do with professional happiness.

For the sake of argument, let's say Mary makes $30,000 a year. While browsing an online job board, she sees a similar position for another organization across town that offers a 15% pay increase. This doesn't sound bad—until you do the math. A 20% increase would give Mary $4,500 more a year, roughly $375 extra a month—before taxes. After taxes, she might have enough to pay for an extra tank of gas and Starbucks every week, exactly what she'll need to cover the extra distance to the new job and back.

This might be enough to push Mary out the door, if she really hates her current job or thinks the boss, Doug, is a huge jerk. If every day is an emotional roller coaster ride that makes her want to jump out of her skin with annoyance and misery, she'd probably be happy to take the new job even with a pay *decrease*. However, if Doug were to give Mary some perks that make her happy, and take away some of the factors that make her miserable, an extra tank of gas isn't going to be enough to lure Mary away from her current job.

"But wait just a minute," you might be saying. "Every single employee I've ever given an exit interview to has told me they quit because of money. Are you telling me they all lied?" The answer is, for the most part, yes. It's no different than the old breakup excuse, "It's not you, it's me." Most people don't want to sit face-to-face with someone and say, "Look, you're an idiot. Just talking to you makes me want to scream, and I probably will do just that if I don't get out here in the next five minutes." Even if an employee does have the nerve to tell you what he or she thinks of you, on a practical level, you might be handy as a reference down the line. So there's major negative benefit in telling the truth. Using money as an excuse is the best way to slip out on relatively good terms.

Money is great, but few organizations can continually (and legally) offer the kind of money that really makes a difference. What they can offer is all the other stuff beyond money that gets and keeps Hundred Percenters and Hundred Percenter hopefuls excited, motivated, and striving to deliver above-and-beyond performance.

One hallmark of 100% Leaders is pragmatism. They take nothing for granted, and they don't stand on ceremony. They find out exactly what their best people want, and if it's practical and possible, they make it happen. They also find out what their folks don't want. If they can't make it go away, they try to neutralize the problem. That doesn't mean trying to mask the negative stuff with perks.

No Such Thing as Average

So what exactly does the average Hundred Percenter want? That's a great question that comes with a loaded answer. I was raised in Buffalo, New York, and even though I now live down south, I remain a die-hard Buffalo Bills fan. I once read that the average NFL player weighs 245 pounds and stands 6'1½''. But when I looked into it, I couldn't find a single player on the Buffalo Bills who weighs 245 pounds or who stands 6'1½''.

I was investigating the reliability of averages for another project, so my curiosity naturally grew. I assigned one of my researchers to scour the rosters of every NFL team, looking for average-sized players. It was pretty tedious work, so I let him stop after 10 teams. As you might guess, he was unable to find even one player who matched the NFL average in both weight and height.

The point of all this is that averages lie. Averages are misleading. Nobody is "average," and if you go looking for the "average" person, you will probably never find him. (Have you ever seen a family with 2.5 kids?) This same "fallacy of the average" holds true when we're talking about Hundred Percenters. What they want—and what they don't want—is as unique and individual as is what *you* want and don't want.

In the book *The War for Talent*, consultants from McKinsey & Company asked thousands of managers and executives, "What are the critical factors in your decision to join and stay at an organization?" The answers were all over the place. Some folks said it's interesting and challenging work; others said it's work they feel passionate about; some said it's career advancement opportunities; others said it's the company's long-term commitment to them. Other popular answers included whether the company is well managed; good relations with the boss; the company's culture and values; the company's physical location; a reasonable work pace; higher pay for high performers; and high annual cash compensation. McKinsey's total list comprised around 40 issues.

Exit interview studies showed similar results. In organization-wide studies, people usually say they quit for reasons that include lack of recognition or rewards; lack of advancement opportunities; lack of feedback from management; not being made to feel like a valued employee; lack of training and education; uncompetitive compensation; and lack of responsibility.

If you can distill these responses into one universal factor that motivates employees to deliver stellar performance, you deserve a medal. We've tried, and it just doesn't work. People are unique, and they are driven by different things. But most organizations still haven't gotten the message. Every day we see companies implement organization-wide strategies that utilize a limited number of motivational techniques to inspire improved performance (desperately hoping to find that "average" employee).

It's not that those "average" techniques don't work; they'll certainly work for some of your employees. But if a patient arrived in the emergency room suffering from 40 stab wounds, are we going to treat only 1 of those wounds and hope that the other 39 will take care of themselves?

Some People Don't Know

One complicating factor we have to address is that there are a decent number of cases where people just don't know what makes them motivated or demotivated. Take Craig, for example. A highly gifted programmer and potential Hundred Percenter, Craig got promoted to manager as a performance "reward." The organization even threw him a party to celebrate the step up. Craig never aspired to be a manager, but with all the attention he got over it, he figured the promotion couldn't be anything but great.

The problem is that while Craig has amazing technical skills, his people skills are pretty lousy, a factor his boss failed to take into account when rewarding Craig for his great performance. Consequently, Craig went from achieving great success as a programmer to experiencing failure after failure as a manager. He started to believe that it was his fault and that he just wasn't good enough. Eventually Craig started thinking about quitting the organization.

Aren't There Any Universal Motivators?

You can't run around giving everybody gift cards or flexible work schedules and expect your people to stay motivated. But there is one thing we all seem to want: a boss who listens to our unique concerns. We want to know someone is paying attention to what gets us revved up, someone who also has the guts to listen to us when we're facing a situation that is emotionally killing us.

It's entirely likely that at any given time many members of your team are going to be motivated or demotivated by a similar set of issues. After all, they share the same boss, and they could be working on the same project or with the same customers. The point isn't that you will never see common motivational themes; it's that even if you do see common themes, those themes could change from week to week, from month to month, from project to project, and from department to department.

There's only one approach that will enable you to reliably and dynamically identify what your people want and what they don't want, the two factors that will inspire them to give—and keep on giving—Hundred Percenter effort. You must engage them in a one-to-one conversation and ask them outright. We call this conversation Shoves and Tugs.

Shoves and Tugs

Everybody has Shoves and Tugs. Shoves are those issues that demotivate you, drain your energy, stop you from giving Hundred Percenter effort, and make you want to quit—they "shove" you out the door. Tugs are those issues that motivate and fulfill you, make you want to give Hundred Percenter effort, and keep you coming back every day—they "tug" at you to stay.

This seems simple enough. But here's the twist: Shoves and Tugs are not flip sides of the same coin. Just because somebody has lots of Tugs coming up this week does not mean he or she doesn't have any Shoves. Before you spend all day trying to figure out how to give people lots of Tugs, you've got to at least acknowledge (and ideally mitigate) their Shoves.

Let me begin with an analogy that's a little out there but that might help clarify this issue. Just as Shoves and Tugs are not opposites, neither are pain and pleasure. The opposite of pleasure isn't pain; it's just the absence of pleasure. Similarly, the opposite of pain isn't pleasure; it's just the absence of pain. If somebody is hitting my foot with a hammer, that's pain. When the hammering stops, that's not pleasure; that's just no more pain. If I'm getting the world's greatest back rub, that's pleasure. When it stops, that's not pain; that's just no more pleasure.

Here's the lesson: If I'm getting a great back rub, that does not preclude somebody from simultaneously hitting my foot with a hammer. If that happens, the pain in my foot will totally detract from the pleasure I'm getting from the back rub. Here's a corollary lesson: If you walk past me one day and see that my foot is being hit with a hammer, you cannot fix the pain in my foot by giving me a back rub. The only way to stop the pain in my foot is to stop the hammer from hitting it.

Every day, in organizations around the world, employees' feet are being hit with hammers, and their bosses' solution isn't to stop the hammer (i.e., eliminate the Shove) but rather to offer a back rub (i.e., offer a Tug).

Consider, for example, a software development team in Silicon Valley led by a manager named Chris. The department was on heavy deadline to finish a new product, and lately Chris's anxiety had caused him to start micromanaging. He began instituting numerous "check in" meetings widely acknowledged as useless and insisting on regular "no-work team lunch hours" that forced high-performing employees to work even later.

The high emotional tension throughout the department was clear to Chris. But rather than ask his team about the source of their frustration, Chris decided to take everyone to Catalina Island for the weekend to relax. He figured it was a great way to offer a nice reward and get everyone's brains back into the game. When he made the announcement, more than a few of the programmers' heads nearly exploded. The last thing they wanted was more time with one another just hanging out and not working. They wanted to finish the project, hit the deadline, and go home to their families. They wanted to stop wasting time at work and just get the job done.

Chris made the mistake of trying to fix a Shove with a Tug, and it backfired. Yes, Catalina Island is beautiful, and perhaps in another circumstance it would have been a nice reward. But his team was getting shoved by too much time away from the actual work of programming, and here comes the boss with a Tug that involves more time away from programming. Not only was the Tug a poor choice, but Chris's credibility is shot; he seems obtuse and insensitive for not understanding what was really demoralizing his team.

When good employees are working with low performers or they're fighting through roadblocks or they've got a terrible working environment—whatever the Shoves may be—it's like getting hit on the foot with a hammer. Great things (Tugs) like autonomy, the ability to have control over an entire process, and the ability to work on innovative projects and teams aren't going to mean a thing until you take away the pain of the Shoves.

What Do You Actually Ask?

A Shoves and Tugs conversation doesn't have to be formal; in fact, it's actually better if it's not. The last thing you want is to make it seem like a performance appraisal. The first rule is, get out from behind your desk. I suggest holding your Shoves and Tugs conversations over coffee or lunch, anywhere two people can have a reasonably private conversation for at least 20 minutes. And just to be clear, we're also talking about a conversation that takes place at least once every quarter (although once a month is even better).

In the majority of cases, two simple questions are all you need to ask:

1. Tell me about a time in the past month or two when you felt demotivated (or frustrated or emotionally burned out or whatever words sound like something you would say).
2. Tell me about a time in the past month or two when you felt motivated (or excited or jazzed up or however you might naturally express this).

Bear in mind that you're not asking these questions simply for the sake of asking questions; you actually want to know the answers. What you'll typically find is that the issues raised by these questions are as different as people's hair color or their choice of ties. Each person is a little bit different, so find out exactly what will drive each individual to jump to Hundred Percenter performance and what is keeping that person firmly lodged in the status quo.

It's natural to wonder if asking these questions will make employees think twice about all the demotivators they face. Could you be putting negative ideas in their heads? Look, just because you have an EKG at a checkup doesn't mean you're more likely to have a heart attack. If you get screened for breast or prostate cancer, it doesn't mean you're more likely to get those cancers.

If you're at risk of a heart attack, getting a good cardiac workup will uncover that hidden risk. It may be scary to learn that your risk is so high (and that's why so many people don't get the necessary tests), but the tests don't cause the illness. So the real question is, do you want to bury your head in the sand, or do you want a team of Hundred Percenters?

Assess the Conversation

How your people answer your Shoves and Tugs questions will provide clues so you can assess how the conversation is progressing and if you need to push for more information.

There are four levels to look for:

1. *Superficial level.* This is when the employee answers, "Everything is fine. I can't think of anything." This person is actively avoiding the issue. We all can point to a

time in the past 90 days when something either pleased us or ticked us off.

2. *Suspicious level.* If you hear a response that sounds like, "I'm sure there are things, but why do you want to know?" it shows the employee is acknowledging an awareness of issues but fears that revealing those issues might result in trouble or even getting fired.

3. *Involved level.* If the employee tells you about a specific problem but offers no recommended solution, there's clear evidence of a Shove. But there is still a level of distrust. Build trust by providing more evidence of how far you are willing to go to fix the situation.

4. *Committed level.* If the employee gives you a full-blown description of a Shove, even if it pertains to you, and tells you specifically what should be done to fix it, you've hit the Shoves and Tugs jackpot.

If you find yourself stuck at the superficial level, it's probably an indication that you don't have a great history with this person. You might get the employee to loosen up a bit if you change the focus to a third-person approach. It's always safer to talk about your own stuff when you pretend it belongs to someone else. To make the shift into third person, ask a question such as:

What are the two to three things you think other employees like best about this organization?

Can you imagine reasons why employees would leave this company?

When your Shoves and Tugs conversation isn't going as well as you'd like, repetition can get it back on track. If you talk to 10 employees and only 1 person tells you a Shove—perhaps the person reports a distaste for being micromanaged, especially on repetitive tasks—you've got something to work with. Let everyone witness your efforts to rein in your tendencies to micromanage. The news of "Wow, she didn't fire me! She actually did what I asked!" will spread fast. The following month, when you have your next set of Shoves and Tugs talks, you'll get a few more employees who will feel safe speaking up. Eventually you'll gain most people's trust.

It takes courage for employees to tell the boss tough things such as, "Well, sometimes you micromanage me, and it really turns me off." And the fact may be that the person describing this Shove needs to be micromanaged from time to time. However, if you come back with a comment like, "Well, if you didn't screw up so much, I wouldn't have to micromanage you," you'll shut down any chance of productive communication. It takes practice to hold your tongue, but a Shoves and Tugs conversation isn't about how you feel or why you (or the organization) act the way you do. For that moment, it's all about the other person. So get used to calmly nodding your head and saying, "I hear you."

There will be Shoves that are outside your control and that you simply can't fix. But don't jump to this conclusion just because you don't see an immediate or obvious way out. Listen to what your employees tell you. The person talking about the Shove is living that Shove and may have some good ideas for how to fix it. If nothing truly can be done to eliminate or neutralize the Shove, be honest about it. Don't lie and say, "Right, well, it might take me six or eight months to be able to swing that, but I'll work on it," hoping that the Shove will be forgotten. As a rule, unaddressed Shoves don't get forgotten; they just get worse.

Before we move on, I want to address one excuse I hear more than any other for avoiding the Shoves and Tugs conversation: "I don't have the time to sit around with all 10 (or 30 or 50—whatever the number) of my employees and talk about this warm and fuzzy stuff." A productive Shoves and Tugs conversation takes no more than 15 to 30 minutes, less time than you probably spend drinking coffee every day. You don't have to talk to every employee in a single day. Talk to one a day, and in a month or so you'll have worked through all 30. And by the time you reach number 30, you'll already have made some progress turning the first 20 into Hundred Percenters.

Shoves and Tugs for Seven Different Personalities

You'll find that certain types of personalities will express similar kinds of Shoves and Tugs. For example, the folks who are always looking for that next adrenaline rush might tell you about Shoves where they felt extremely bored or where they were stymied in their attempt to implement some new cutting-edge improvement. Or people who love solving problems might tell you about Tugs like salvaging projects that others have abandoned. Similar personality types won't have exactly the same Shoves and Tugs, but the similarities you do hear can help you better prepare for your Shoves and Tugs conversations.

There are hundreds of theories on personality types, but when it comes to workplace behavior, we've found there are seven driving needs that influence who people are and what they like and dislike:

1. Achievement
2. Power
3. Affiliation
4. Security

5. Reward
6. Adventure
7. Actualization

Let's take a look at how all seven come into play through a study of seven employees, all of whom hold senior marketing positions at StayHealthyInc., an international (fictional, but based on our real-life research) fitness franchise. All seven subjects are around 40 years old, they all have kids, they all drink coffee, they're all married, they've all tried Atkins and South Beach diets, they all went to college and graduate school, and they are all potential Hundred Percenters. These folks are pretty demographically similar, but that doesn't mean they're motivated or demotivated by the same things.

Achievement

Grace is a risk taker whose excitement about the job increases as her responsibilities grow. She focuses on giving superior performance, but isn't overly invested in getting recognition for her work. Repetitive or menial work easily frustrates her and decreases the effort she gives to the job. Grace will always choose going solo over being in a team unless she is partnered with someone who is just like her.

People like Grace, with a high need for achievement, seek to excel. Predominantly achievement-motivated individuals avoid low-risk situations because the easily attained success is not a genuine achievement. These individuals prefer work that has a moderate probability of success. Achievement-motivated individuals want regular feedback in order to monitor the progress of their achievements. They prefer to work either alone or with others like themselves (see Table 4-1).

Table 4-1 High need for achievement

Common Tugs	Common Shoves
Difficult tasks	Tasks that are repetitive or too easy
Lots of feedback	Tasks with no measurable outcome
Praise	Working with low performers
Evaluations	
Working alone	
Working with other achievers	
Getting to choose tasks or work or projects	
Becoming a "specialist" at a task or job	

Power

Sue needs power, usually in the form of control. To some people, she can come off as bossy and territorial, but she's very competent. When she's in control, she's highly motivated. If she lost that control, she'd lose her desire to work for StayHealthyInc.

Folks like Sue need personal power. They want to be in charge, and they crave the authority to make decisions that will impact others. The need for power also means wanting to be well regarded and to be followed. Power-motivated individuals typically do not respond well to being told what to do or how to do it—unless it comes from a person they wish to emulate (see Table 4-2).

Table 4-2 High need for power

Common Tugs	Common Shoves
Responsibility	Micromanagement
Recognition	Fuzzy organizational
Making clear the path to	structure
advancement	Shared decision making
Job titles	
Leading projects	

Affiliation

Everyone knows Rory. He's a team player, and nothing motivates him more than improving organizational systems, solving problems, and finding new opportunities to work in a group environment. He's got a gift for infusing coworkers and clients with positive energy and for pulling people together to achieve a common goal. If you give Rory a project where he might step on some of his coworkers' feet, don't be surprised if he passes.

Employees like Rory have a high need for affiliation. They want harmonious relationships, and they want to feel accepted by other people. These individuals prefer work that provides significant personal interaction. They enjoy being part of groups and make excellent team members, though sometimes they get distracted by the social interaction. They can perform particularly well in customer service and client interaction situations (see Table 4-3).

Table 4-3 High need for affiliation

Common Tugs	Common Shoves
Teamwork	Solo work
Jobs with much social contact	Isolation
Face-to-face time	Office physically distant
Committees	from others
Extracurricular activities	

Security

Paul is driven by having a clear job role and taking on only sure bets. He doesn't want rapid change or high-risk opportunities. If it hasn't been done before or if he can't see it in writing, he's not interested. If you invite Paul in on a project by saying, "I'm not sure how you fit into this team yet, but come on board and we'll figure it out as we go," you're going to send him scurrying for safety.

Paul and others like him have a high need for security and look for continuity in their work life. They may prefer to stay with the same company, or in the same position or department, for the long haul. They are driven by guarantees. High-security people get anxious over change. They value consistency in their job, work, and pay (see Table 4-4).

Table 4-4 High need for security

Common Tugs	Common Shoves
Contracts	Risk
History (few layoffs, low	Rapid change
turnover, etc.)	
Clear job role and duties	

Reward

Candice works efficiently and produces the best results when she knows what's in it for her. If you put her on a team with coworkers who don't pull their load but will get the same reward, her motivation decreases rapidly.

Employees like Candice, who have a high need for reward, are looking for the tangibles they can accumulate through their work. They want to know how much they can earn and how they can earn it. They want to know how they will be compensated for their time and effort. And they need to have it spelled out clearly. High-reward people like to see that effort and compensation are clearly aligned, and they typically don't like systems that reward time in a job over effort in a job (see Table 4-5).

Table 4-5 High need for reward

Common Tugs	Common Shoves
Pay for performance Incentives Perks Praise Recognition	Pay for time Low performers with same pay

Adventure

Christine is an adrenaline junkie and needs to do interesting and cutting-edge work. If there's a new or experimental project, she's all over it. She doesn't much care for stupid people and thus often works by herself. Give her a risky project with lots of autonomy, and she's ecstatic. Put her with a large group of mediocre minds doing boring work, and she's ready to take a header off her cubicle wall.

People like Christine have a need for adventure and are motivated by risk, change, and uncertainty. They thrive when the environment or the work is constantly changing. They tend to like challenges and jump at the opportunity to be the first to do some-thing new. They don't mind failure, especially if given the chance to try again. High-adventure people often go out on their own. They may be entrepreneurs or freelancers. They are likely to change jobs and companies often, especially when they get bored or feel that they have maxed out their potential somewhere (see Table 4-6).

Table 4-6 High need for adventure

Common Tugs	Common Shoves
Difficult tasks New tasks and jobs Change Being "the first"	Repetitive tasks and jobs Easy or simple tasks and jobs

Actualization

Bill is driven by a need to feel good about himself and the work he does. Last month he worked on a project that developed creative ways to increase teaching about healthy living and eating in the public school system, and he was more driven and productive than he'd ever been.

Folks like Bill, who have a need for actualization, focus on a desire for self-fulfillment, namely the tendency to reach their own greatest potential. They want to maximize themselves in the world through their job. High-actualization people tend to concentrate more on their own goals than on the goals of a company—although those goals can be aligned (see Table 4-7).

It's critical that when you pitch anything important to your people, you gear it directly to the individual needs of the type of person you're dealing with. Your actualization people probably aren't

Table 4-7 High need for actualization

Common Tugs	Common Shoves
Setting own goals Focusing on personal growth Looking at how current job fits with future plans Participating in continuing education, seminars, etc.	Lack of opportunities for personal growth Micromanagement

looking for a whole lot of power, nor will your reward people be overly interested in the social connections your affiliation people want. Your security-focused people will not want the adventure angle (and vice versa). People driven by security don't want to hear what an exciting risk this is and how no one in the industry has ever before attempted this kind of move. Adventure people don't want to hear how proven the concept is (they want to be on the cutting edge). And so on. The real key is to listen carefully to your Shoves and Tugs conversations and then, coupled with what you now know about these common personality types, frame your solutions in a way that's tailored to the person sitting in front of you.

Taking Action

As you meet with each employee, jot down clear and simple lists of that person's Shoves and Tugs. First, examine the Shoves, the issues that need fixing. If it appears that getting rid of a Shove will help make someone a Hundred Percenter, then do whatever it takes (within reason) to eliminate or neutralize the Shove. You may hear some Shoves that are endemic to you as a leader, and if they are valid, remain open to making some personal adjustments. Dealing with the Shoves must come before the Tugs because remember, you have to stop hitting people's feet with a hammer before they can enjoy the back rub.

Once you've eliminated the critical Shoves, take the same approach with the Tugs. Find issues you can tackle that will help create Hundred Percenters, and just get going. Keep in mind which of the seven personality types you are dealing with, and address employees with the specific types of words and actions they want to see and hear.

Putting It Together

Because the Shoves and Tugs that every leader will face are going to be significantly different, I can't supply you with a one-size-fits-all motivator. However, what I can do is show you how Leo, the director of marketing for StayHealthyInc., addressed the Shoves and Tugs of all seven of the employees we visited with earlier. First, Leo mapped out each employee's Shoves and Tugs and then came up with individual action plans. Let's take a look.

Grace

Grace, as you may recall, has a high need for achievement. Leo invited her to meet over coffee, and she expressed real excitement when he asked about her motivators and demotivators from the last month or two.

"I'm really glad you asked that, Leo, because I'm worried that some of the work I'm doing isn't going to help us hit those HARD Goals you set last month.

"Like that proposal I gave you last month. We could be driving so much more traffic to the website if we had an upgraded virtual shopping system. I know memberships are our key focus, and they bring in a lot of revenue, but we've got some great products that rival the competition. Only no one knows about them. I know how to turn this around; I just need the chance to prove it."

Grace was committed to giving Leo the information he was after. Because she's a good employee with a strong work ethic, she's not likely to ask for something as unreasonable as being released from all menial tasks in order to chase wild and unpredictable chances. However, she did let Leo know she'd like a little more time to focus on more challenging work. And because Leo is familiar with the seven driving needs and because he recognizes Grace as having a personality type that is focused on achievement, he was able gain a deeper appreciation of their conversation.

After giving the situation some thought, Leo again met with Grace to discuss what he could do regarding her Shoves and Tugs.

"I reread your proposal, Grace, and I agree that while some of it is risky, the payoff could be worthwhile and help us hit our HARD Goals. Now, I do still need you on the budget work and the internal assignments. However, I potentially could open up about 15 to 20% of your time, given that your other work stays consistently strong.

"I'm not saying your proposal will automatically fly. I need to see some big preliminary results before I can bring this before my boss. So how about this: I'll give you three months with some focused time on this project. I'm going to need weekly progress meetings, and we'll need to see adequate progress. After three months, if you're meeting the criteria that you and I will lay out together, I'll get you a meeting with the folks who have the power to approve the next steps. I still need you to pull the same load around here, but I'll give you a chance to make this happen."

Sue

The next day, Leo met with Sue, who likes to have power and control. When Leo asked Sue about her Shoves and Tugs, she was not quite as forthcoming as was Grace.

"I don't know, Leo. I mean, it's all part of the job. What's this about anyway? Is there something going on I need to know about?" Sue was suspicious of Leo's intentions and leery of revealing her thoughts in case it got her in trouble. Despite Leo's reassurance that there would be no negative repercussions, Sue stayed tight-lipped. Leo chatted pleasantly for five minutes and then called a friendly halt to the meeting. He decided it would be best for Sue to observe how he addressed other employees' Shoves and Tugs over the next few weeks. He hoped it would encourage her to open up the next time they met.

When they met in a month, Sue, while still a bit hesitant, was more open to talking.

"I don't mean this with any disrespect, Leo, and I'm hesitant to even say anything. But sometimes I feel just a little too monitored, like you don't think I can do the job. And if that's the case, I'd like it if you would tell me what I need to do better. You said you believed that I could hit those HARD Goals, and I believed you, and I'm working hard to develop the new skills I need. I love this company, and I'd like to hang in for the long run and to earn my way up the ranks. But I need to know that I have your trust that I can do the job."

Leo felt a bit ruffled when Sue implied that he was a micromanager. But he kept things in perspective and was able to see that, due to Sue's penchant for power, it might actually push her to greater performance if he were to pull back a bit when it came to managing her. Leo is hopeful that with a little less monitoring Sue will start to produce the Hundred Percenter effort he knows she's capable of.

Rory

Next, Leo met with Rory, the guy who likes everyone and wants to be liked back. Given his affiliation personality type, Rory was a little hesitant to tell Leo anything that might sound harsh or cause waves. Because Leo understands Rory's driving needs, he quickly turned his line of Shoves and Tugs questioning to a third-party focus, allowing Rory to speak his mind under the guise of bringing benefit to the whole team. That was all it took to get Rory talking.

"I know I'm not the only one who sometimes feels isolated in my work. And I think for us to hit our HARD Goals, more teamwork would be really beneficial. I've talked to a lot of people who really liked it the time you assigned us to that No Homework Team, where we all got together and worked together until the job was done. It was so different from our usual approach of meeting, then working alone, then pulling all the pieces together. I think people would really respond if we did more of that kind of team thing."

Leo has a special interest in addressing Rory's Shoves and Tugs. Not only is Rory a talented employee who has great potential to reach Hundred Percenter status, he's also an influencer. A lot of other employees look to Rory for guidance. Leo knows that kind of power can go a long way in getting folks to see the benefit in giving Hundred Percenter performance. If Rory gives the thumbs-up, Leo's job becomes infinitely easier.

Luckily, Rory isn't asking for anything over the top, as is typically the case. Hundred Percenters, or those with potential to be such, will rarely overstep the bounds when asked about Shoves and Tugs.

After listening to what Rory had to say, Leo immediately responded.

"I could see where more teamwork could be effective. I'll tell you what, Rory, I'll try the No Homework approach again if you're willing to put together the agenda and help lead the meeting. If it goes smoothly and you can show me some solid evidence to back the results, we'll try it again. Then you and I will sit down and measure the effectiveness of this approach and how and when it best fits our needs. I can't promise you every meeting is going to be like this, but if it brings results, yeah, we'll work it in."

Paul

Paul is all about security and no-risk assurance of success. When he sat down with Leo, he was definitely on the borderline of superficial and suspicious when it came to talking about his Shoves and Tugs.

"Everything's fine, Leo. I have no complaints. I'm really happy here."

Leo then encouraged Paul to talk about his Shoves and Tugs in the third person by saying "Then maybe you can tell me a few things you think other employees like and dislike about the organization." Paul remained hesitant, but he did open up a little.

"Well, I have heard a few things. You know, like we're wasting a lot of time doing work that isn't going to help us hit the department's HARD Goals."

This didn't give Leo a whole lot to go on, and so he pushed Paul to divulge more information. "Can you give me some examples of this, Paul?"

"Well, I know last month when we were working on strengthening the brand image, it was really hectic. A bunch of us put in a lot of overtime, often doing stuff that wasn't really productive but that I suppose needed to get done. But it got really stressful."

Leo nodded his head and said, "This is good for me to know, Paul. Look, you're in there working with everyone. Do you have any ideas for how we can make things better?"

"Yeah, actually I do. Part of what's killing us is the rush to produce the Monthly Analytics report. We need the report, but the way we have to rush it out for that crazy deadline every month means we're wasting huge time waiting for other areas because they don't have their data finished. And then, because they aren't on time with their data, the data aren't entered into the central data-base, which means the whole process is totally manual, which is a killer. And the worst part? The executives don't even read the report until two weeks later at their Executive Roundtable meeting. One of the guys in IT told me that if we waited one extra week until all the data were loaded, the report would take 30 minutes to produce rather than two weeks, and we'd have it done in plenty of time for the executives' meeting. You wanna know what really keeps me up at night? The whole report is so rushed and manual and cobbled together, I'm in a cold sweat that the numbers are wrong."

Leo was learning that once you get folks talking, not only will they tell you their Shoves and Tugs, but they'll outline the exact steps necessary to fix them. Leo asked Paul, "Are you willing to do a little work to discover why that arbitrary deadline was originally set that way? And are you willing to write up everything you just said into a couple of paragraphs so we can try to fix this process, which seems really broken?" Paul's eyes lit up when he replied, "Seriously, honest-to-goodness process improvement? Consistency, predictably, and accuracy? Man, I'm all over that."

It took a little time conversing, but Leo was able to get Paul not only to admit what was shoving him into unhappiness, but to volunteer what would tug him toward greater performance. Even better, Paul was willing to do the legwork to make his Tug a reality.

Candice

Candice is inspired to work hard when she knows there is a tangible reward. She's already seen Leo's efforts in action addressing her coworkers' Shoves and Tugs and she's happy to have a chance to talk to Leo herself.

"I'm so glad it's finally my turn. I think it's great you're doing this, and I love that I finally have a boss who cares. I know you sort of kicked us in the rear a bit with those new HARD Goals, but I appreciate that we're aiming for something really worth hitting. The thing I want to talk to you about is my performance on hitting those goals. I'm really trying, but I constantly feel like I'm missing the mark. I don't think I really understand the measurements for our pay-for-performance program. Last month I handled that huge problem with our biggest vendor and did the kickoff for five new gyms, but I didn't see anything for my efforts. I'm really confused."

While it may seem that Candice is only out for what she can get, Leo knows that her reward-motivated personality gets jumpstarted by the promise of compensation. And while Leo isn't about to hand her something for nothing, he quickly sees a way to turn Candice's admission about her Shoves and Tugs into a strategy for pushing her to Hundred Percenter performance.

"I think it's great you want to aim higher, Candice, and I'm happy to help. I think we can start solving this. What do you say we meet tomorrow, for about 30 minutes, and really dig into the measures in the performance plan and look at where you've been at for the past few months. Let's make sure everything is clear, and we can talk about any parts that don't make sense. We'll come up with a few goals and some strategies to achieve them, and we'll give you the next week to see what you can do. Then we'll meet again next week and compare notes. You tell me what it was like, and I'll give you my feedback on what I saw. Together, I feel confident we can get you on track to where you want to go and in the right direction of our HARD Goals."

Christine

Christine seeks adventure and hits Hundred Percenter performance when her adrenaline is running strong. The Shoves and Tugs she set before Leo didn't surprise him at all.

"Some of the work is really repetitive, and while I understand it has to get done, I just wish once in a while there was something more. It would make the menial stuff more tolerable. I don't want to come off sounding like a complainer, because I am really happy. I just want some bigger challenges, and I'd really like to be involved in some of the really tough parts of the HARD Goals."

Leo understands that adventure and change is what drives Christine to achieve. He admits that it's been a while since he gave her a big challenge and that he could potentially lose a valuable employee if he doesn't do something soon to address her Shoves. The good news is that he's putting together a task team, and Christine is more than capable of leading it. Leo makes it clear that the job comes with very tough targets, but he knows with Christine, the harder he pushes, the more she'll achieve.

Bill

Finally, Leo met with Bill, who is driven by actualization, a need to keep growing. Bill had heard from the others about how these meetings were going down, and so he was prepared to talk about his Shoves and Tugs.

"The thing is, Leo, I feel kind of lost. I like the job, but I just don't feel any sense of direction or where I'm going with it all. Lately it's like I show up, do my work, and go home. I'm just not learning anything; my brain's kind of atrophying."

Leo knows it's to his advantage to help Bill chart out his future and recognize the opportunities where he can really push himself to grow and develop.

"I can understand your frustration, Bill, and I can definitely help you find your way. These new HARD Goals are going to require us to learn some things we don't presently know how to do. I've got some projects I think will stretch your brain. I'd welcome the chance to meet with you and discuss them. I could do it as soon as tomorrow, say one o'clock; we'll we meet for an hour and start to map out a plan to really stretch you."

Conclusion

Shoves demotivate employees and stop them from giving 100% effort. Tugs motivate employees to give 100% effort and to stay with the organization. Tap into these intrinsic employee motivators and demotivators with monthly one-on-one conversations that ask, "Tell me about a time in the past month or two when you felt demotivated or motivated (or excited or jazzed up, etc.)." Probe deeper if answers are superficial, suspicious, or involved, and work toward reaching an ideal, committed response such as, "Here's the problem and here's how we can specifically fix it." Shoves must be neutralized or mitigated before Tugs can have any real impact.

5

Hiring for Attitude

Leadership IQ's Hundred Percenter Index Questions

This organization hires people that have the right attitude to be high performers.

This organization hires people that have the right attitude to fit our culture.

Introduction

When most leaders and managers talk about "hiring the right people," they mean the folks who can do the tasks of the job. But that's out of step with what the latest research tells us is important to hiring success. For instance, one of our studies tracked 20,000 new hires in a comprehensive range of industries over 18 months.

Within that first year and a half on the job, the total failure rate of those new hires (including those who got fired, received poor performance reviews, or were written up) was a whopping 46%. And 89% of the time, these newly hired employees failed for attitudinal reasons, namely: coachability, emotional intelligence, motivation, and temperament. Skills barely made the list at 11%. Out of the employees who did make it past 18 months, only 35% became middle performers, and only 19% went on to become legitimate Hundred Percenters.

Most organizations already have the tools to hire for skill. Virtually every profession has some kind of a test that assesses technical ability. If you want to be a board-certified neurosurgeon, you have to pass a test. If you want to be a Cisco Certified Internetwork Expert (considered to be perhaps the toughest networking certification), you have to pass a written test and a lab test. If you want to be a nurse, pharmacist, engineer, nuclear physicist, car mechanic, or whatever it may be, there's a test to determine if you have the skills to do the job. Even though I personally lack the skills to pass the tests for any of those jobs, I could easily proctor the exam. And if I buy the scoring key, guess what? I could grade those tests as well. And so could you.

We know how to hire for skill, but what most organizations lack are the tools to hire for attitude. 100% Leaders recognize that all the skills in the world don't mean a thing if an employee stirs up conflict, refuses to be accountable, and won't listen to leadership. These exceptional leaders have redefined how today's organizations hire, and Hiring for Attitude is allowing a rapidly growing number of organizations to enjoy greater hiring success. Companies are asking new kinds of interview questions that provide real information about attitude instead of the vague or canned answers many traditional hiring questions produce. And there are now answer keys that allow accurate rating of a candidate's answers even across hiring panels and multiple interviewers. Now you'll be able to hire the most technically gifted employees who also have a fantastic attitude that's a perfect match for your organization.

It all starts by identifying your Brown Shorts, a wacky term that pays homage to great companies like Southwest Airlines and UPS, two organizations that have used actual brown shorts to help them select the folks best and least suited to work in their cultures. For the rest of us, Brown Shorts is just shorthand for the specific high-performer and low-performer attitudes that make our organization different from everybody else's.

Let's take a look at how it all works.

What in the World Are Brown Shorts?

We know Hundred Percenters possess "great fit" attitudes that complement the culture of the organization for which they work. And we know that in most industries, the majority of new hires fail due to a lack of coachability, emotional intelligence, motivation, and temperament. But there's no one-size-fits-all solution when it comes to Hiring for Attitude. The key attitudes that define an organization's success are unique. An employee who is competitive and individualistic may be the perfect fit for a solo-hunter, commission-driven sales force or Wall Street financial firm. But put that same personality to work in a collaborative, team-loving start-up culture with a bunch of programmers all coding around one big communal desk, and that individualistic superstar is doomed to fail.

Southwest Airlines is one organization that knows its winning attitude (fun), and every employee—from executives to pilots to flight attendants—lives it. That's because Southwest does a great job of assessing attitude when they hire. If you've ever heard the cabin crew sing the seat-belt instructions, you've experienced the Southwest attitude of fun. There's even a customer-created Face-book page named "Funny Stuff They Say on Southwest Airlines" where Southwest customers can share their personal favorite South-west fun experiences.

Fun is Southwest's competitive advantage; it's how the organi-zation gains customer loyalty and ensures repeat business. Fun is also how they load planes quickly and why their customers don't mind the absence of seat assignments. Given that the organization just recorded its thirty-ninth consecutive year of profitability—in a business sector where profits are really tough to make—I'd say they're doing fun right. But not all fun is alike. Southwest wants a certain kind of fun, a specific attitude, and in order to find people who share it, they've come up with some pretty clever (and often unconventional) tools to help them assess whether or not a candi-date has "it."

A former Southwest executive once told me a story about a group interview Southwest held when they were hiring pilots. To give a little background on pilots here, you need to know that lots of them are male, over 40, ex-military, with a pretty serious demeanor that shows in everything they do, including how they dress. So these candidates were conscientiously attired in black suits, white shirts, black ties, black socks, and spit-polished black shoes. As the story goes, they are all ushered into a typically bland meeting room where everybody sits down and waits for the usual drill. But then along comes the Southwest interviewer who says, "Welcome! And thanks for coming to Southwest Airlines! We want y'all to be comfortable today, so would anybody like to change out of their suit pants and put on these brown shorts I've got here?"

Now remember that this is a job interview. You know—those hyperformal affairs in sparse meeting rooms that precisely follow standard scripts where you just talk about all the great things you did at your last job and why you want this new job. That's it. No getting undressed and putting on shorts or anything crazy like that.

Understandably, a good number of the pilots were taken aback. After all, there they were, all dressed up in their best black suits, white shirts, black ties, black over-the-calf dress socks, and spit-polished black shoes, and someone is asking them to change into in some ugly brown shorts? "Find some other chump to look like a fool," was probably the thought going through most of their heads.

And that was just fine with Southwest. Because the only candidates they were interested in were the ones who were happy to wear the brown shorts. All the others, even if they had been Top Gun pilots, were told "thank you" and sent home, allowing Southwest's interviewers to quickly get to work interviewing only those candidates who showed the right attitudinal potential (fun) to be a high performer at Southwest. The company's cofounder and former CEO, Herb Kelleher, wasn't kidding when he said, "If you don't have a great attitude, we don't want you." (See Figure 5-1.)

Figure 5-1 Are your candidates a good fit for your Brown Shorts?

If you're thinking this all sounds a little extreme, consider this: Let's say the average pilot flies 75 hours per month, and the average flight is roughly 2 hours long. That comes to about 38 flights per month per pilot. If a typical Boeing 737 holds about 140 passengers and flies about 75% full, that's about 105 passengers per flight. If you then multiply that by the roughly 38 flights each pilot flies per month, that's just under 4,000 passengers (i.e., customers) a month with whom a Southwest pilot might interact. That's a whole lot of customers who could be lost if Southwest hired a pilot with a bad attitude. I don't care how many billboards you rent and television spots you buy, all the marketing in the world can't help you if your employees are undermining your brand every day.

If you're interviewing for a job at Southwest, don't expect the shorts. This is just one example of how the organization hires for attitude. One of our salespeople recently flew Southwest and talked to a pilot who said he was asked to try on a clown suit at his initial interview. The point of all this is to explain the term *Brown Shorts* and to demonstrate why it's important for every organization to have a similar test of attitude—something as simple and effective as a pair of brown shorts—to assess which candidates have the "right" attitude and which ones have the "wrong" attitude.

Finding Your Brown Shorts

Southwest can sum up its culture neatly and quickly in one word: *fun*. Many other top-performing organizations such as Ritz Carlton, Disney, Google, and GE can also define their cultures in one or two words. But most organizations aren't there yet; it takes time. Here's how to get started finding your organization's Brown Shorts.

Discovering Differential Characteristics

The key to discovering your Brown Shorts is Differential Characteristics—the attitudes that truly separate your high performers from your middle performers and your low performers from everybody else. You don't want a giant list of every possible attitudinal characteristic under the sun; you just want the important critical predictors of employee success or failure for your organization.

In theory, this shouldn't be a complicated process, but in practice, things sometimes get off track—like when someone at the organization downloads a long list of "great to have" attitudes from the Internet. Characteristics like honesty, integrity, emotional intelligence, work ethic, positive attitude, loyalty, values, mission focus, innovation, teamwork, persuasion, effective communication, and so on. Then they pass the list around to all the hiring managers and say, "Please choose the characteristics that you think are most important for our employees to have." If your HR department or senior executives asked you to pick from a list of important characteristics, wouldn't you choose integrity, honesty, and values? And it's not like you can leave teamwork, work ethic, or positive attitude off the list. My point is that when everything is important, nothing is important.

Discovering your Brown Shorts is not about making a list of all the characteristics that sound really nice or all the traits you wish you had. This is an exercise in realism, not idealism. You need to know two things here: First, what characteristics predict failure in your organization (so you can avoid hiring anyone who possesses those characteristics)? Second, what characteristics predict success in your organization (so you can recruit and hire more folks who have those characteristics)?

Ultimately, you're going to end up with a list of three to seven Positive Brown Shorts (characteristics that differentiate high from middle performers) and three to seven Negative Brown Shorts (characteristics that differentiate low performers from everyone else). It's this short list of key attitudes that will direct how you create your Brown Shorts Interview Questions and Answer Guidelines. First, though, you need to complete the Brown Shorts Discovery process and find out exactly what your Brown Shorts are.

Brown Shorts Interviews

If we had perfect data from performance appraisals, we wouldn't have to dig much further to understand our Brown Shorts. We'd already know exactly which people were struggling or failing in their jobs, why it was happening, what attitudinal problems were most prevalent, and which ones were least correctable. We'd also know whether these attitudinal problems were systemic or specific to certain individuals. And if the only people who received high ratings were people with both great skills and great attitudes, we'd know exactly what they were doing and what great attitudes differentiated them from everybody else. Unfortunately, attitudes are seriously underrepresented on most performance reviews, and we all know plenty of people getting top reviews who don't really deliver top performance.

This is why discovering your Brown Shorts requires interviewing some of the folks who are living your culture and regularly interacting with both your high and low performers. When Leadership IQ partners with companies on Brown Shorts projects, our interviewers start at the top (with the CEO, if possible) and then work their way deeper into the organization, step by step. You'll want to do the same, creating a rough draft of your Brown Shorts as you go.

The gist of what you'll ask in these interviews is simple: "In your experience, what separates our great attitude people from everyone else in the organization?" That's a really broad question, though, and one that a lot of people struggle to answer. So start your interviews by being more specific. You might ask something such as: "Think of someone in the organization who truly represents our culture. This would be our poster child for having the right attitude for our organization. Could you tell me about a time this person did something that really exemplifies having the right attitude? It could be something big or small, but it should be something that made an impression on you."

The goal here is to get specifics, and that means pushing for details. You may have to ask multiple questions, multiple times—following up each time with the question, "Could you give me another example?" Once you've exhausted that line of questioning, start on the inverse version. Try something like: "Without naming names, think of someone who works (or worked) in the organization who doesn't represent the culture. This would be our poster child for having the wrong attitude for this organization. Could you tell me about a time this person did something that exemplifies having the wrong attitude? It could be something big or small, but it should be something that made an impression on you." As the interviews progress, you'll begin to identify trends in the feedback you get. Similar points will pop up from interview to interview, and your Brown Shorts will start to take shape in a rough draft form.

Getting to the Front Lines

Employees on the front lines are typically closer to your new hires, making their perspective on who will and won't succeed an important one. It becomes more difficult to conduct phone or in-person interviews in organizations of more than 70 people. In these situations, online surveys tend to work the best, but you do have to conduct them differently than you did the executive interviews. With employees, you're not asking about the people who work for them. You want to ask them about themselves and their colleagues.

You're also not starting with a blank slate like you did with the CEO and other executives. You have all the data collected in the executive interviews, and you should now have an emerging picture of your Brown Shorts. What you want to obtain from the folks on the front lines is validation and more specifics so you can bring that Brown Shorts picture clearly into view.

The survey for your frontline employees will consist of somewhere between 6 and 10 open-ended questions. The best questions—that is, the ones that elicit the most detailed responses—are the ones built around the rough draft Brown Shorts you've already developed.

Imagine that your executive interviews uncover a major attitudinal problem, something that really defines the low performers. Perhaps the problem is an unwillingness to learn new skills on the fly, and, more specifically, to take on the responsibility of learning those skills. In this case, we might include a question on the employee survey such as, "Please describe a situation when you were asked to do something work related that you didn't know how to do."

Questions like this one give you specific answers to help you develop and finalize your Brown Shorts Interview Questions (and the Answer Guidelines you'll make later). You can also ask questions that will confirm that you've understood the issue correctly. For example, if your executive interviews reveal that bad attitudes generally involve reacting poorly with customers, but the nature of the poor reactions is still unclear (or the descriptions cannot be categorized), your question could be, "Please describe a recent mistake that you've seen other employees make in their dealings with customers." Questions like this will help clarify the range of issues you deal with and help flesh out the specifics you need to develop your Brown Shorts.

When you're finished with all the interviewing and surveying, what you'll have is an amazingly deep understanding of the attitudes that do and don't work in your particular culture. Almost every time we deliver a Brown Shorts report to our clients, we get feedback that sounds something like "I think you understand our culture better than we do (at least before we got the report)." And usually, they're right. The Brown Shorts Discovery process is that revealing.

The Interview Questions You Shouldn't Be Asking

Now before we take all that great data and create our Brown Shorts Interview Questions, we need to eliminate some of the less effective interview questions so we have room for the good ones. Many interview questions are utterly useless, and some are flat-out dangerous. Some questions have a built-in design flaw whereby they elicit replies that are rehearsed or gamed. As a result, they deliver skewed data that can negatively impact your hiring decisions. The following four categories represent the kinds of bad interview questions that Leadership IQ surveys and studies have found to be the most commonly used across a broad spectrum of industries. If you (or your organization) currently use any of these types of questions, it's important to understand why they are so bad and to immediately stop using them.

#1: Don't Ask Questions Like "Tell Me About Yourself" or "What Are Your Strengths and Weaknesses?"

These are bad interview questions for a variety of reasons. First, these questions are too vague, allowing only for vacuous answers. Second, because these questions are so well known, and because it's remarkably easy to conceive of and verbalize any number of rehearsed answers to them, virtually every candidate has a canned answer ready, such as "I work too hard" or "I care too much" or "I have a perfectionist streak." Third, because all those rehearsed, vacuous answers sound the same, it's nearly impossible to differentiate future high and low performers based on any of the answers.

A fundamental test of the effectiveness of an interview question is the extent to which it differentiates high and low performers. If reports started rolling in that interviewers were asking "What are your weaknesses?" and hearing responses such as "I have a violent temper, and I stalked my last boss" or "I hate people, and I can't stand taking orders," then perhaps this line of questioning would be valuable. But honest responses such as these are rarely heard in an interview, and the odds are small that anyone will answer any of these three questions with complete honesty.

#2: Don't Ask Leading "Behavioral" Questions

Behavioral questions can predict future behavior, but most of these questions lose effectiveness due to wording. For example, consider this popularly asked behavioral question: "Tell me about a conflict with a coworker and how you resolved it?" This question is fine up until ". . . and how you resolved it." This leading phrase signals the candidate to skip over any mention of all the times she failed to resolve conflicts with coworkers. What if she resolved a conflict 1 time but failed to resolve conflicts 500 times? That's important hiring information.

For all the infinite variety of personalities and attitudes out there, you can still roughly categorize people into two groups: the "problem bringers" and "problem solvers." When you ask a problem bringer about a problem, you'll hear about the problem and nothing more. By contrast, when you ask a problem solver about a problem, you'll hear about the problem, but you'll also hear some solutions. That's because problem solvers can't even think of a problem without instantly generating possible solutions. For them, separating problems and solutions is as ludicrous as separating wet from water. Leading questions rob you of the opportunity to find out if someone is a problem bringer or a problem solver.

#3: Don't Ask Hypothetical Questions

Most hypothetical questions begin by asking: "What would you do if . . ." followed by some kind of situation such as "you had to make a big decision?" Hypothetical questions are problematic because the answers they inspire are usually idealized. You'll probably get a lot of responses that sound like something a high performer would do, but those answers will only sometimes reflect reality. Despite what we might like to believe about ourselves, there's a huge gap between our hypothetical selves and our real selves.

#4: Don't Ask Undifferentiating Questions

How many golf balls can fit in a school bus? This question isn't the setup for a bad joke; it's actually one of the interview questions on the infamous list "15 Google Interview Questions That Will Make You Feel Stupid," a bunch of goofy brain teasers that Google now publicly acknowledges are silly and that they have banned from their interview process. If you ask an interview question and you have no clue how to use the answer as an indicator of high and low performance, what's the point of asking it?

I once had an executive from a well-known energy company tell me that his hiring managers regularly ask, "If you could be any kind of animal, what animal would you be?" The top executives decided, without any scientific study, that future high performers would say "tiger" and future low performers would say "elephant." And they really stood by those answers. If you didn't say tiger, you were unlikely to get hired. Just imagine how many potential high performers they've passed over (and how many low performers they've hired), all because of an answer to an undifferentiating question.

The lesson here is that smart companies and 100% Leaders recognize that the fundamental test of an interview question is whether or not it differentiates high and low performers. Pseudopsychological questions may be fun to ask. But without scientific evidence to correlate the answers with real-life work behaviors (such as proof that folks who answer "500,000 golf balls" are guaranteed high performers and those who say "100,000" are doomed to low performance), these types of interview questions fail the test.

Bad interview questions can be crazy, funny, and even illegal, but they all share a common link: they don't help you to assess attitude. For that you need Brown Shorts Interview Questions, so let's get started learning how to create them.

How to Create Brown Shorts Interview Questions

Your Brown Shorts Discovery process allowed you to dig deep into your organizational culture. You should now have a list of the critical high- and low-performer attitudes that predict success and failure in your organization. The Brown Shorts Interview Questions you're about to create will present candidates with Differential Situations that are selected specifically around those attitudes. Using these custom-built questions, you will surreptitiously pressure candidates to abandon their prepared answers and carefully rehearsed scripts. What you'll hear instead is the raw truth about how they really reacted to particular attitude-based situations in the past. Once you measure their responses against the real-life performance of your best (and worst) people (using your Answer Guidelines, which I'll show you how to create next), you'll have a clear picture of what each candidate would be like working for your company.

Creating Your Brown Shorts Interview Questions: A Four-Step Process

Creating your Brown Shorts Interview Questions couldn't be easier. You're simply going to follow the four-step process found in Figure 5-2 for each question you create:

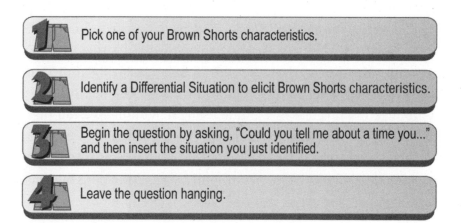

1 Pick one of your Brown Shorts characteristics.

2 Identify a Differential Situation to elicit Brown Shorts characteristics.

3 Begin the question by asking, "Could you tell me about a time you..." and then insert the situation you just identified.

4 Leave the question hanging.

Figure 5-2 Four steps to create Brown Shorts Interview Questions

Let's walk through the four steps individually.

Brown Shorts Interview Question Step 1: Pick One of Your Brown Shorts Characteristics

The first step is choosing one of the Brown Shorts characteristics you identified during your Brown Shorts Discovery process. For example, let's imagine that we've conducted interviews with leaders and employees at Company X. Table 5-1 summarizes the results of that Discovery process with a list of Company X's Positive Brown Shorts (attitudes that differentiate their high performers) and Negative Brown Shorts (low performer attitudes that just don't fit their culture).

All Company X needs to do to complete Step 1 is to choose one of these Brown Shorts characteristics.

Brown Shorts Interview Question Step 2: Identify a Differential Situation to Elicit Brown Shorts Characteristics

It's clear when you contrast the Positive and Negative Brown Shorts listed in Table 5-1 that high and low performers at Company X respond very differently in situations such as facing problems, receiving credit, responding to significant changes in the workplace, working cross-functionally, and learning new skills. We call these "Differential Situations" because they're the moments where the differences between high and low performers are most starkly contrasted. This contrast is what you want, because situations in which high and low performers respond similarly are of no use in determining attitude.

Step 2 requires identifying a Differential Situation in which your high performers will reveal their great attitudes and low performers will reveal their bad attitudes. For Company X, a Differential Situation could be, for example, when employees are given

Table 5-1 Company X's Positive and Negative Brown Shorts

Positive Brown Shorts	Negative Brown Shorts
Collaborative. I extend help without being asked and without expectation of recognition or reward.	*Self-Focused.* I expect individual recognition and something in return for my hard work even if it was a team effort.
Strong Other Awareness. I share my constructive thoughts and reactions without making my colleagues defensive, angry, or embarrassed.	*No Other Awareness.* I want my ideas heard regardless of how they may belittle, embarrass, or anger my colleagues.
Accountable. I am responsible for the quality and timeliness of my work. I look for solutions and share my learnings with others so everyone can learn.	*Blamer.* When things go wrong I am frequently heard saying things like: "I couldn't get it done because . . ." or "It's somebody else's fault . . ."
Self-Directed Learner. I adapt to change and seek out the resources I need to gain the skills and knowledge my job requires.	*Negative.* When faced with new situations, I immediately look for the reasons why they won't work. Change is rarely a good thing.

an assignment they don't know how to do or when they're asked to do something outside their job description or when they lack the skills required to complete an assignment.

Once you've got some Differential Situations to work with, simply choose one of them and build a Brown Shorts Interview Question around it. I'm personally partial to the situation where folks have faced failure, but when you create these questions in your organization, you should pick the situations that your employees face most frequently.

Brown Shorts Interview Question Step 3: Begin the Question by Asking, "Could You Tell Me About a Time You . . ." and Then Insert the Differential Situation You Just Identified

The third step is to begin with the phrase "Could you tell me about a time you . . ." and then finish the question by inserting the Differential Situation you just identified. Asking "Could you . . ." instead of the usual "Tell me . . ." softens questions, makes the interview more conversational, and encourages candidates to be less guarded so they reveal more information about their true attitudes. So Company X's Brown Shorts Interview Question would be something like "Could you tell me about a time you lacked the skills required to complete an assignment?"

Brown Shorts Interview Question Step 4: Leave the Question Hanging

The final step is to leave your Brown Shorts Interview Question hanging. Similar to the problem we identified with most behavioral questions, the addition of phrases such as ". . . and how did you overcome that?" or ". . . and how did you solve that challenge?" makes your

Brown Shorts Interview Question a leading question and destroys its effectiveness. We simply want to ask "Could you tell me about a time you lacked the skills required to complete an assignment?" and leave it at that. Resist the urge to add "and what did you do?"

The specific words you select and how you choose to say them does matter in interviewing. You can't read from a bad script and expect that you're going to make great hires. This is a battle where subtlety matters, small words make a big difference, and your performance is critical. That's why Leadership IQ has a Hiring for Attitude certification program. It takes more than 15 minutes to do this really well.

Examples of Brown Shorts Interview Questions

The following are examples of Brown Shorts Interview Questions:

Could you tell me about a time you were asked to change the way you do something?

Could you tell me about a time you showed personal leadership?

Could you tell me about a time you were asked to do something you didn't know how to do?

Could you tell me about a time you made a mistake?

Could you tell me about a time you taught a wide variety of learners?

Could you tell me about a time you worked on a team to achieve a goal?

Could you tell me about your most significant learning experience?

Could you tell me about a time you joined an already
  established team?

Could you tell me about a time you set and missed a learning
  goal?

Could you tell me about a time—separate from performance
  appraisal—when you got feedback?

Could you tell me about a time you experienced professional
  growth?

Could you tell me about a time you faced competing
  priorities?

Could you tell me about a time you had difficult interactions
  with a colleague or customer?

Could you tell me about a time you thought outside the box?

Could you tell me about a time you lacked the skills or
  knowledge to complete a job?

Brown Shorts Interview Questions Are Open to Interpretation

You probably noticed that Brown Shorts Interview Questions are
open to interpretation. For example, consider the question "Could
you tell me about a time you thought outside the box?" I could
have an idea that I think is outside the box but that someone else
would consider stodgy and inside the box. That same idea could
be way too far outside the box at a more conservative organization. It's all in the eye of the beholder—and dependent on your
unique corporate culture.

Asking Brown Shorts Interview Questions that are open to
interpretation provides a clear view of the candidate's standards.
I could ask somebody an open question such as "Could you tell me
about your proudest accomplishment this year?" If the response is

"I showed up for work on time more than half of the days," well, I just learned that this person has very low standards when it comes to pride. But if somebody else answered "Even though I received 28 patents and doubled the size of the company, I'm not ready to feel proud because I really should have done more," I just learned that this person has really high standards when it comes to pride.

The Brown Shorts Answer Guidelines you're about to create will help you correctly interpret the responses you get to your Brown Shorts Interview Questions. But before we create your interview answer key, we first need to review the Coachability Question.

The Coachability Question

At the start of this chapter I cited a Leadership IQ study that revealed a lack of coachability as the single biggest reason why new hires fail. In all the work Leadership IQ has done in designing Brown Shorts interview processes for our clients, we've never seen an organization where coachability wasn't a pertinent and valuable characteristic.

The Coachability Question, combined with your Brown Shorts Interview Questions, reveals information about a candidate's coachability with the level of detail you want. The Coachability Question has five parts, and each part must be asked in order and exactly as I describe it here:

1. What was your boss's name? Please spell the full name for me.
2. Tell me about [name] as a boss.
3. What's something that you could have done (or done differently) to enhance your working relationship with [name]?

4. When I talk to [name], what will he/she tell me your
    strengths are?

5. Now everyone has areas where he or she can improve, so
    when I talk to [name], what will he/she tell me your
    weaknesses are?

Here's how each step works.

Coachability Question Step 1: Make Them Believe You're Going to Talk with Their Previous Boss

The Coachability Question begins by asking "What was your boss's
name?" Sometimes when candidates are presently employed, they
don't want to share that name; in those cases, just go with the name
of the boss from the candidate's previous job.

Once you've got the name (e.g., Kate Johnson), get the spelling
by asking "Please spell the full name for me." This creates a situation where the candidate believes you're actually going to call
Kate, which provides added motivation to give more truthful information during the interview.

This simple step is the one that interviewers try to skip. The
common misconception is that because it's a short step, it's incon-
sequential. I know it's outside what most interviewers do, and it
can feel somewhat uncomfortable. But The Coachability Question
will not work if you don't confirm the spelling of the name. This
little psychological twist is what makes this whole process so
revealing.

It's also important to use the language I've given here: "Please
spell the full name for me." Note that this is not exactly a question, but rather a stated request. It's pretty formal language (more
formal than "How do you spell that?") and signals seriousness on
your part about contacting that boss.

Coachability Question Step 2: Ask Them to Describe Their Boss

Here you simply ask, "So tell me about what Kate was like as a boss." The candidate's response will provide clues about what this person is looking for in a boss. If the answer is "Kate was very hands-on and wanted regular updates," stated in a clipped manner and with a hint of a frown, you can pretty safely infer that this candidate doesn't like that style of management. If someone indicates (either implicitly or explicitly) that he doesn't respond well to micromanagers, and you're a bit of a micromanager, you need to ask yourself whether you could successfully manage this person. But if someone's last boss sounds like you, and it appears the candidate loved working for that person, then that's a good sign.

If you don't get a complete response on the first try, try one of these probing questions:

What's something you wish Kate had done more of?
What's something you wish Kate had done less of?

Many people have been coached not to speak about former bosses during job interviews. These two probes usually manage to skate under the typical interviewee's defenses because they're not asking directly about the boss, but rather about what the employee could have used more and less of from that boss in order to have been more effective on the job.

Coachability Question Step 3: Ask What They Personally Could Have Done Differently

Everyone has the potential for improvement, even Hundred Percenters. This question takes that a step further and asks whether or not someone feels personally accountable for making that improvement happen. Step 3 also reveals whether or not the candidate takes any ownership for creating and maintaining a healthy relationship with the boss. The best candidates will not only tell you about the ownership they've taken but also about the personal changes they've made since working with that boss. High performers don't just talk about what they could do to improve; they actually go and do it.

Coachability Question Step 4: Ask Them What Their Boss Considered Their Strengths

Asking: "When I talk to Kate, what will she tell me are your biggest strengths?" has two purposes. First, before you start asking about someone's weaknesses, it's nice to start with a more pleasant question. Talking about strengths makes people feel less guarded, and it will help keep your candidates feeling comfortable and open in their communications with you.

Second, it gives you an honest look at the qualities your candidates like best about themselves. Remember the interview questions you shouldn't ask that we covered earlier? When we directly ask people to describe their strengths, it typically results in canned or rehearsed answers. But when you ask it this way, with the added pressure that you're likely going to verify this with the candidate's last boss, you'll hear a very different and truthful answer.

Coachability Question Step 5: Ask Them What Their Boss Considered Their Weaknesses

Asking "Now everyone has some weaknesses, so when I talk to Kate, what will she tell me yours are?" is perhaps the most critical part of the five-step process, but it only works if you've completed the previous four steps. When you do the first four steps successfully (especially confirming the spelling of the boss's name in Step 1), you'll likely be shocked at the level of honesty Step 5 elicits.

Listen to the responses you get to both Steps 4 and 5 on two levels. First, assess whether the strength or weakness is a Positive or Negative Brown Shorts characteristic this person shares with your current high and low performers. Remember, the focus of The Coachability Question is to determine if someone is coachable or not.

Second, if the response you get is "I can't think of any weaknesses," or something like "I honestly don't know what Kate thought about me," then you've hit upon the biggest Warning Sign that someone is not coachable. If that person didn't (or couldn't) hear the constructive feedback offered by a previous boss, what are the chances that you'll be successful giving that person feedback? People who can't hear and assimilate constructive criticism are not coachable. And even without formal conversations with their boss, if they can't put themselves in their boss's shoes and anticipate their assessment, they're not coachable.

Creating Brown Shorts Answer Guidelines

The concept of using Answer Guidelines as part of the hiring process is revolutionary in the world of hiring. Leadership IQ is the only group I know that teaches this technique. But what is the point of administering a test (and hiring definitely is a test where failure delivers serious consequences) without the ability to correct that test? And yet, managers everywhere are doing just that when they interview without an answer key.

Two big problems occur when organizations hire for attitude without using Answer Guidelines. First off, you can usually find something you like, and something you dislike, in virtually every person you interview. (Of course, given that the consequences of hiring a bad attitude are worse than not hiring a good attitude, I'm more concerned about the former). So without having some foundation to orient us and to tell us what good and bad answers sound like, it's awfully hard to evaluate candidates consistently and correctly.

The second big problem is the extent to which everybody involved in your hiring process does (or does not) understand your Brown Shorts. It may seem absurd, but there are a lot of people in your organization, including leaders, who really don't know, or can't articulate, what makes your culture special. Just as they can't clearly tell you what separates your high and low performers.

Hiring for Attitude requires both your Brown Shorts and your Brown Shorts Interview Questions. But in order to make it all work, you also need your Brown Shorts Answer Guidelines. That way, when you (and every member of your hiring team) are in the middle of a live interview, you'll know exactly what you should be listening for and how you should react when you hear it.

Answer Guidelines reflect how your current high and low performers answer your Brown Shorts Interview Questions broken into two categories: high-performer Positive Signals and low-performer Warning Signs.

Here's the approach we take at Leadership IQ when an organization brings us in on a Hiring for Attitude project. We first discover the organization's Brown Shorts and then use that insight to craft the Brown Shorts Interview Questions. We then make a few strategic tweaks to those questions so they sound less like a job interview and more like an opportunity to help. Then we include the tweaked questions in an online survey that gets sent to the organization's employees. Note that we typically use a carefully selected sample of employees, and we use a statistical method called a power study to determine how many respondents we'll need for the survey.

Implementing the survey may get a bit technical, but the underlying idea is quite simple: you're testing your Brown Shorts Interview Questions and asking employees to tell you what good and bad answers sound like. This significantly increases the odds of picking out the future high performers and avoiding the low performers.

Here's a sample from one organization's Answer Guidelines for the Brown Shorts Interview Question: Could you tell me about a time a boss gave you tough feedback?

Warning Signs
These types of answers can indicate a poor fit with the organizational culture.

- I never got feedback from that boss; it was more like you get a task and you just do it at that job. I never heard any complaints about my work, though, so I feel confident I was doing a good job.
- Most of the time the feedback was probably related to my lack of patience: I am not someone who likes to sit around and wait for things to happen. I am a go-getter with a strong work ethic. So my boss would say, "You need to be more patient with the people who just don't 'get it' as quickly as you do," things like that. And, of course, I would politely accept the feedback and agree to try.
- He had plenty to say on what I was doing wrong, but he never once gave me the direction or tools to do better.
- The only way to make it at my last job was to be a "yes" person. You just did as you were told and never questioned it.
- It was confusing to me because I thought I did a great job, but my boss thought I could have done better. I don't think it was possible to please him.

Positive Signals

These types of answers can indicate a good fit with the organization's culture.

- I had to really push past what I thought I could do in order to achieve what my boss said he knew I could do. It was sort of scary, but also really exciting, and he was right; I did a great job, and it actually led to a small promotion for me.

- Within the first three months of working there I was put in charge of rolling out an initiative for the entire department. There were a lot of deadlines and regulations to follow, and because I was new I did not have a lot of strong relationships. So it was extremely difficult to get buy-in and confirmations from my peers. I kept going to my VP to let him know what was going on. One day he nicely pointed out to me a sign he had hanging in his office that read, "If you are going to come to me with problems, come to me with the solutions too." I got it after that, that I needed to come up with possible solutions before I took my challenges to leadership, and even if my solutions were not accepted, they could be a springboard for brainstorming how to make something happen rather than just having a pity party.

- I was willing to adapt because I saw how making the changes my boss suggested would benefit the client, the organization, and me.

- My direct manager had a vision that was really different from mine, and I think we both had good and valid ideas. But when I saw that he was not going to change his mind, I jumped on board with him and did everything I could to drive his vision to completion. It actually worked out really well. I still wonder sometimes if my idea would have worked, but I feel ok about changing course and doing what had to be done to take care of the immediate challenge.

One thing that's critical to note here is that these examples are all actual answers from real employees at real organizations. You're going to hear some tough feedback as you talk to your people too, so be prepared for the kick-in-the-gut feeling that says, "These are the real answers from people to whom I pay money every week."

Scoring the Answers

Your Brown Shorts Answer Guidelines allow you to more accurately assess who's most likely to succeed or fail in your unique organization based on candidates' answers to your interview questions. You can find a free rating form at http://www.leadershipiq .com/wp-content/uploads/2012/01/LeadershipIQ_Candidate _Rating_Form.pdf. This form can easily be merged with any existing form you use so you can rate your candidates' answers against your Answer Guidelines.

What Does the Final Score Mean?

Because our rating form uses a 7-point scale, typically, a score of 1 to 3 indicates a candidate who should immediately drop out of consideration. (To learn the statistical reasons why we use a 7-point scale, read our white paper titled "Why 5-Point Scales Don't Work and

Other Deadly Sins of Employee Surveys" found at leadershipiq.com.) This low score is a clear indication that the candidate shares at least one (and maybe more) big characteristic with your low performers—and it's probably a Talented Terror. Discussing it further isn't going to make that person magically turn into a good cultural fit; it's just going to deplete your mental energy.

With all other candidates, simply average all the scores together. The candidate with the highest score should be your first choice (assuming that person passes all your other hiring tests).

I would be concerned if your best scores are only in the 4 to 5 range. You really want to see your best candidates rating a final 6-point-something or even a 7. So if you're finding that the most candidates are mediocre fits—not awful, but not great—it's a sign that there's probably something broken in your recruiting process.

One question we often hear during our Hiring for Attitude certification training is, "What if there are several of us doing the interviews and our scores vary?" Well, right now, with your current system, your evaluations probably do vary. That's why we have the Brown Shorts Answer Guidelines. You already conducted the analysis about what constitutes good and bad answers. That's your guide. Any discrepancies after the interview should immediately be brought back to that guide so that "it" can settle the debate. Your Answer Guidelines hold the answers about who will, and won't, succeed.

Conclusion

We started this chapter by reviewing our research that tracked 20,000 new hires and found that 89% of the time new hires failed, it was for attitudinal reasons, not lack of skill. Most organizations know how to hire for skill, but they have no test by which to assess attitude, and many have no concrete idea of what the attitudes they should be hiring for even are. You can train for skills and technical competence; but you can't train for "attitude." 100% Leaders recruit, interview, and Hire for Attitude.

Hiring for Attitude consists of: (1) Discovering the unique attitudes your organization needs to hire for your Brown Shorts, (2) Eliminating bad hiring questions that don't assess attitude so you can ask Brown Shorts Interview Questions instead, and (3) Making sure interviewers know what great and bad attitude sounds like by training them with your custom Answer Guidelines. Executive interviews and a survey of current employees will help you identify your Brown Shorts and create your Answer Guidelines. And Brown Shorts Interview Questions are easily constructed with this simple four-step process: (1) Pick one of your Brown Shorts characteristics, (2) Identity a Differential Situation that elicits Brown Shorts characteristics, (3) Begin by asking, "Could you tell me about a time. . . ." and insert Differential Characteristic, and (4) Leave the question hanging.

The five-step Coachability Question addresses the number one reason why new hires fail and reveals what it will really be like to work with, and to manage, each candidate.

There are bad interview questions that you definitely want to avoid, but there's no such thing as a bad interview answer, as long as it's an honest answer that tells you something about attitude. Get the real data you need to make good hiring decisions by discovering your organization's Brown Shorts and building a hiring process (that includes an answer key) around them.

6

Word Pictures

Leadership IQ's Hundred Percenter Index Questions

Actually practicing this organization's values is critical to my success here.

This organization has clearly defined what behaviors are necessary to achieve success here.

Introduction

Here's a statistic that should make every leader cringe: only 29% of employees say that their organization has always (or almost always) clearly defined what behaviors are necessary to achieve success. Meanwhile, roughly 50% of employees say the opposite (i.e., that the organization has never, or almost never, defined those behaviors).

The resulting amount of lost productivity and misguided activity is staggering. But there's a natural tendency among some managers and executives to resist these statistics. After all, how is it possible that employees don't know the specific behaviors we want them to exhibit? Shouldn't this be basic knowledge?

Why Don't Employees Already Know This Stuff?

Employees don't know enough about what behaviors are necessary to achieve success for two reasons. First, some companies don't believe they should have to teach it. Second, some companies aren't doing a good enough job effecting knowledge transfer—their teaching isn't getting through.

Regarding the first issue, I've had executives look me right in the eye and say, "I shouldn't have to spoon-feed people information about what behaviors are necessary to achieve success here; they should just know it." When I hear that I think, "If you're truly doing a perfect job of hiring people with great attitudes who already understand everything you want and can deliver it, then I suppose you can skip the detailed teaching." And that's true. If 100% of your employees are demonstrably high performers and you have 0% preventable errors (no defects, service breakdowns, or missed handoffs), then you can confidently skip the whole teaching/coaching concept as well as this chapter. But how many of us can truly say that? And, ironically, the companies that could be excluded are only that self-assured because they already do such a good job of teaching high and low performance.

Lots of companies just aren't teaching performance expectations well enough. I'm reminded of a behind-the-scenes football show about an NFL team during training camp. There was a scene with the third-string quarterback (who you just knew was going to get cut) asking the coach, "What can I do to get better?" To which the coach replied, "Just keep doing what you're doing."

The quarterback was pretty frustrated with the coach's answer. He didn't articulate his frustration well, so here's a distillation of what he said: "What I'm currently doing has made me a third-string quarterback! What should I do differently so that I can become second string or even first string?"

I recount this story because I see this same kind of scenario over and over again when I'm working with managers. "Keep doing what you're doing," they tell their people. To which any employee could justifiably respond, "Well, what I'm doing just got me put on a 90-day improvement plan, so have you got anything a little more specific?'

The Struggle to Be Specific

Here are some examples of common euphemisms, admonitions, and clichés that pass for performance expectations in far too many organizations:

High performing employees will:

Maintain the highest standards of professionalism.
Treat customers as a priority.
Regard responsibility to the patient as paramount.
Demonstrate positive attitude and behavior.

Lead by example.

Engage in open, honest, and direct conversation.

Respect and trust the talents and intentions of their fellow employees.

Challenge the company's thinking.

This kind of fuzzy language populates our performance appraisals, codes of conduct, mission statements, and more. In fact, every one of these examples came from a real company. But such statements don't really count as teaching or setting clear expectations.

Let's do a little comparison. Imagine that you're trying to get your employees to be more accountable, so you decide to set better performance expectations. Following are two different ways to do this. The examples are excerpted from two companies' performance appraisals, although both versions were also used in other training and employee orientation formats. After all, if you're going to hold employees accountable for certain behaviors, it only makes sense that you would use those same behaviors to constantly and continuously teach employees about your expectations.

After you read both versions, I think you'll be able to see which company does a better job of setting expectations—and thus teaching employees—about accountability.

Version #1

This performance appraisal tool uses fairly common language in standard paragraph format to define accountability. For purposes of its performance appraisal, this company provided paragraphs, like the following one, on a variety of topics. It then asked managers to rate employees (on a scale of 1 to 5) on the extent to which employees exemplified these behaviors. It's all standard stuff that you find being done in any number of organizations.

As an employee, I am considered accountable when I take responsibility for my own actions and decisions. I keep to my commitments, and when that's not possible, I notify the appropriate person and develop a Plan B. I act as a role model for accepting responsibility and being accountable, and I encourage others to do the same.

Version #2

Contrast the traditional paragraph in Version #1 with Version #2 (shown in Table 6-1), which defines accountability in three ways. The left column (Needs Work) describes the behaviors associated with someone who is not being accountable. The middle column (Good Work) describes an acceptable level of accountability, and the right column (Great Work) details the behaviors associated with a fantastic level of accountability. (Note: I condensed the original descriptions in all three columns to provide a more succinct example.) For performance appraisals, managers simply identified which employees belonged in which categories.

Now let's compare Version #1 and Version #2. Which of the two will likely do a better job of teaching employees what we mean when we say "be accountable"? I've used these examples and asked this same question of countless audiences, and the answer is always unanimous: Version #2 is the more effective teaching tool.

Version #2 demonstrates Word Pictures. It is effective by design—created specifically to be a great teaching tool—and we use it in many facets of Leadership IQ training. When used correctly, the Word Pictures technique clears up any performance misconceptions and shows current employees how they can better exhibit the high performer behaviors you want. It's the difference between saying "Go out and be accountable" and giving employees specific and highly visual behavioral information that shows

Table 6-1 Performance appraisal Version #2

Needs Work on Accountability	Good Work on Accountability	Great Work on Accountability
When new changes are implemented, I resist and push for a return to the status quo. I encourage others to reject and protest change as well.	I openly support change initiatives, and I find opportunities to help complete projects more quickly and effectively.	I do everything in the Good Work category, plus I encourage and convince my fellow employees to support change initiatives.
When breakdowns or missed communications occur, I engage in finger-pointing and blaming others.	I accept personal responsibility for quality and timeliness of work without making excuses or blaming others.	I actively redirect conversations with my colleagues to stop them from making excuses or blaming others.
When I make mistakes or miss deadlines, I offer excuses like "I couldn't get it done because. . . ." When the going gets tough or intense, I become frantic and overreact.	If it looks like I won't personally be able to meet a commitment, I take responsibility for implementing an alternative that ensures the commitment still gets met.	I immediately remedy problems and errors and work with others to develop root-cause solutions that prevent the same problems or errors from reoccurring.
I avoid extra work, and when working in a team, I allow my coworkers to do most of the work.	I willingly accept extra work, and when working in a team, I support my teammates when they need my help.	I seek out incomplete work that I can tackle. My teammates often compliment me for my group support and for how I go out of my way to ensure that every team member gets deserved recognition.

what accountability actually looks like when employees are demonstrating it. Word Pictures don't leave attitude open to interpretation. They paint a clear picture of what those attitudes look like using behaviorally specific words.

Why Are Word Pictures So Powerful?

Word Pictures have two very important characteristics that make them effective: behavioral specificity and concept attainment.

Behavioral Specificity

Word Pictures are exactly what the name suggests, and they're so powerful because they apply behavioral specificity. You're going to paint a picture, with your words, of the specific behaviors you want to see. Your employees, upon reading these vivid words, will be able to envision themselves exhibiting the behaviors just as the words describe. To that end, Word Pictures use the same three tests of behavioral specificity we applied to our Brown Shorts in Chapter 5, "Hiring for Attitude":

Could you identify the specific behaviors in each category?
Could two strangers observe those behaviors?
Could two strangers grade those behaviors?

The toughest part about creating Word Pictures is making them specific enough to pass the observable and gradable tests. But Word Pictures must pass these tests to be effective.

Concept Attainment

The categorical distinction of Needs Work, Good Work, and Great Work represents the second powerful aspect of Word Pictures.

Word Pictures are based on a scientifically robust learning theory called concept attainment. In a nutshell, concept attainment involves learning through studying positive and negative examples. Do you remember the Sesame Street song "One of These Things (Is Not Like the Others)"? Well, that song actually uses some advanced cognitive psychology—concept attainment. For example, to teach you about the characteristics of a square, Grover or Big Bird has you look at a bunch of squares (the positive examples). But there's one triangle (the negative example) hanging out in the middle of all those squares. Or you learn about the characteristics of an apple by looking at apples (positive examples) and then at an orange, banana, or pear (negative examples). By analyzing those positive and negative examples, you very quickly figure out the characteristics that define squares and apples.

Research tells us that we learn the characteristics of apples faster and more thoroughly with concept attainment than we do if we listen to a lecture on the characteristics of apples. Concept attainment can also be applied to performance-related learning. While a great deal of research shows people can learn by being told how to do something (positive examples), those same studies show that people learn even more when they're also told how *not* to do something (negative examples). Or, as the poet William Blake said roughly 200 years ago, "You never know what is enough unless you know what is more than enough."

Some of the greatest lessons you learned as a kid (and that you probably teach to your kids) are negative examples. Here are a few negative examples I've uttered to my kids in the past few days:

Don't touch the hot stove.
Don't put that thing in your mouth.
Don't hit your brother/sister.
Don't pick your nose.

Don't stand in the hallway without clothes on.

Don't talk with your mouth full.

Don't take such a big bite.

Don't touch the clean laundry with those grimy hands.

Don't jump on the clean laundry.

Don't stand on the furniture.

Don't stage dive off my new chair.

I also offer positive examples, but if you've ever taught by negative example, you know how effective it is. Using the cognitive psychology of concept attainment, we've discovered that employees learn a lot faster and more completely when they understand both what you want and what you don't want. Great teaching is not an either/or thing; it requires both positive and negative examples. Word Pictures are designed to provide both.

We do a lot of work with textual analysis at Leadership IQ, and one thing you'll notice is that the Word Picture example in Version #2 uses first-person pronouns ("I do" instead of "you do" or "she does"). Using first-person pronouns helps the people reading your Word Pictures paint a better mental picture. They can more clearly imagine themselves engaged in those specific behaviors. Thus, each of the categories is kept behaviorally specific and distinct.

By the way, most of us learned about concepts like first-person pronouns with concept attainment—positive and negative examples. You learned the definition of a first-person pronoun by seeing positive examples (*I* or *me*) and negative examples (*you*, *she*, *he*, or *they*). We learn many things through concept attainment. In fact, if you pay attention to the positive and negative examples that you see in the next few days, I guarantee you'll be amazed at how many things you learn through concept attainment. Whether we plan for it or not, this kind of learning happens all the time. And once you realize what a great tool it is, you'll do that "I could've had a V8!" head slap and wonder why you haven't used Word Pictures for employee training before.

Word Pictures Work for Any Topic

Word Pictures are a scientifically advanced method for teaching employees, and you can teach virtually any performance topic with them. Some of the performance related Word Pictures we've created for our clients include: accountability, customer service, leadership, service excellence, ownership, responsibility, problem solving, creativity, collaboration, teamwork, open-mindedness, communication, innovation, leading by example, professionalism, confidence, leading change, discipline, initiation, emotional intelligence, patience, perseverance, purpose, trust, respect, shared values, meeting challenges head-on, exceeding expectations, efficiency, passion, fun, individual growth, analytical thinking, persistence, organization, commitment, courage, openness, dependability, focus, motivation, transparency, expertise, compromise, delegation, competition, accommodation, reward, abstract thinking, outcome focus, credibility, truth seeking, diversity, flexibility, tenacity, entitlement, achievement, critical feedback, proactivity, and problem solving—just to name a few.

The topics you choose to present to your employees in Word Pictures are entirely up to you. But one of the keys to effective teaching is maintaining the interest of the people you're teaching. People learn best when they are inspired, challenged, and stimulated. And while Word Pictures certainly meet those requirements, don't inundate your people with too many Word Pictures. Using Word Pictures to teach everything under the sun causes employees to grow apathetic and stop learning entirely. So choose your topics carefully.

Word Pictures for Leaders

Word Pictures can be used for any topic, even at the leadership level. One of our clients, an insurance company, discovered that its leaders were struggling with giving feedback to employees. (When we conducted an employee engagement survey, their people had pretty low scores on the Hundred Percenter Index questions "Constructive feedback from my leader has helped me to improve my performance" and "My leader holds people accountable for their performance.") So we gathered a group of managers and together created a Word Picture for "giving feedback." Table 6-2 illustrates the results.

There's a lot to like about this organization's Word Picture, but here are a few of my favorite aspects.

Under the Needs Work heading, the company specified some of the behaviors that were actually taking place regularly such as:

- I wait weeks and sometimes months to address issues, and then I deliver diluted feedback.
- I make tough feedback easier to hear by keeping it vague or by sugarcoating my words.
- How employees choose to act on critical feedback is up to them. It's not my job to help them create a plan for improvement.

What's interesting is that before Word Pictures, nobody ever said to these leaders, "That's bad behavior. Stop doing it." Oftentimes, just the act of labeling a behavior as "bad" or "good" immediately increases or decreases the incidence of that behavior. The label Needs Work makes it crystal clear that these are ineffective techniques that should be stopped immediately.

Table 6-2 Word Picture for "giving feedback"

Needs Work	Good Work	Great Work
Negative feedback is all I give, and I give it frequently as it's the most effective way to get employees to perform.	My feedback is specific and direct, and I try to stay objective and to consider employee input and needs.	I give behaviorally specific feedback often, and I stay facts-focused when discussing issues or problems with employees.
I wait weeks and sometimes months to address issues, and then I deliver diluted feedback.	I address employee issues as they happen whenever possible.	I always deliver feedback in the moment and while the facts are fresh.
How employees choose to act on critical feedback is up to them. It's not my job to help them create a plan for improvement.	I make my feedback goal oriented and measureable when possible so progress can be easily tracked.	I deliver consistent feedback including areas of opportunity for improvement and growth via weekly face-to-face employee meetings.
Of course some employees feel criticized or offended by my words. Negative feedback is supposed to be tough.	When it's convenient, I deliver feedback with face-to-face communication.	I exercise excellent listening skills and show genuine concern and care when delivering feedback.

Table 6-2 Word Picture for "giving feedback" (*continued*)

Needs Work	Good Work	Great Work
I give positive feedback even when undeserved. It helps build confidence and self-esteem and makes employees like and trust me more.	I tailor feedback so it meets individual needs. When it's possible, I give clearly defined goals and expectations and provide examples of positive behavior.	I custom tailor feedback always including clear and measurable employee goals, specific directions, and clear examples of what high- and low-performer behavior looks like.
Feedback is not the time to invite two-way conversation. A lecture style— "I talk, you listen" —approach is best. I typically don't hear about bad news until well after it happens.	I listen to employee input about feedback when it's offered. I typically hear bad news as it happens, so I feel pretty confident that employees feel safe coming to me with problems.	I invite two-way conversation and openly seek employee opinions and feedback in problem solving. Employees regularly tell me they feel safe talking to me about their problems.
I make tough feedback easier to hear by keeping it vague or sugarcoating my words.	I try to stay focused on facts and solutions whenever I give feedback. Sometimes I lose my cool.	I never look to blame. I focus on preventing errors from recurring and on finding solutions.

I also really like these examples from the Great Work category for the behaviorally specific picture they paint:

- I deliver consistent feedback including areas of opportunity for improvement and growth via weekly face-to-face employee meetings.
- I custom tailor feedback always including clear and measurable employee goals, specific directions, and clear examples of what high- and low-performer behavior looks like.

Start with Your Culture

Too many organizations take the Word Pictures concept and try to teach every attitude under the sun. They create a long list of attitudes such as "We want everyone to show commitment, efficiency, sensitivity to customers, a sense of humor, class, and great teamwork." But, for example, if your organizational success isn't a result of teamwork, if yours is a more individualistic organization, then don't try to teach teamwork. Instead teach individualism. Identify the attitudes that are your competitive advantage and that are most important to your culture, and focus your Word Pictures there. These are the most important attitudes you can teach employees.

Needs Work are the behaviors you want to see eliminated. These are the manifestations of bad attitude that cause real trouble. Good Work is exactly what it sounds like: the behaviors that ensure the work gets done right and on time, but there's still room for improvement. And then Great Work is superstardom. This is what the Michael Jordan equivalent of great behavior in your organization looks like.

We've found that in the average organization, there are typically 10 to15% of employees in the Needs Work category, some 70%-ish in the Good Work category, and somewhere between 10 to 20% in the Great Work category.

Word Pictures provide every employee with clear performance guidelines. Performance levels are described vividly, with observable behavior that is gradable. So we can sit down with employees and say, "Look here at this Great Work category. You came close, but here in the Needs Work category, these specific behaviors are what stopped you from being a superstar." Even better, employees can use Word Pictures to self-correct, where they say to themselves, "I came close to being a superstar, but here's where I went wrong, and here's what I'll do next time so I do hit that Great Work level."

Word Pictures are also verifiable and explicit. These are not behaviors that require 20 years of experience and in-depth knowledge of the corporate history. Define your Word Pictures so any employee, whether an executive or working right on the front lines, can easily understand and visualize exactly what you're talking about.

Word Pictures in Action: Caesars Entertainment Corporation

Caesars Entertainment Corporation is the largest casino entertainment company in the world. It owns and operates casinos, hotels, and golf courses under brand names that include Harrah's, Caesars Palace, Bally's, Paris, Rio, Flamingo, and the Imperial Palace. It has more than 60,000 employees and is committed to hiring for—and teaching—attitude. Even in the midst of the global recession, Caesars Entertainment continued to reach new customer satisfaction benchmarks.

Caesars Entertainment is a great organization, so I was delighted to head to Las Vegas when Terry Byrnes, vice president of total service, gave me a call. (Plus, hanging out in Las Vegas at Caesars Palace is not exactly a hardship.) Terry is well known and respected in the service world and has developed numerous innovations for delivering sophisticated customer service.

Terry and his team had assessed untold hours of mystery shopper video and knew exactly where service breakdowns occurred. They had also diagnosed their customers' psychological state at every stage of their visit—from entry to exit and every game, show, meal, and rest in between. Caesars' customer satisfaction metrics and predictions are world class; the team knows precisely how much more, or less, customers will spend depending on how delighted they were on their last trip.

On top of all that, Terry had assessed 30 properties around the country and knew exactly what separated high performers from everyone else. He knew that the organization's Brown Shorts were built around a concept of ownership. High performers across the Caesars properties take ownership of delighting customers (and anticipating their preferences and needs); knowing the answers to the most important guest questions (where everything is and what's going on); initiating interactions; and delivering service with quality, accuracy, and speed.

Terry had revolutionized the science of total service. Now he wanted an equally innovative technique for embedding these practices more thoroughly in the Caesars culture.

He immediately loved the science behind Word Pictures. His first thought was that this was a great way to stamp out some of the behaviors that were undermining performance. As good as Caesars is, there are 60,000 employees out there, and some of them are not going to be performing at the highest levels. When that happens, guest satisfaction drops, which in turn means suboptimizing financial performance. According to Caesars' CEO, a spending increase of only $5 per guest (about as much as a fancy coffee) in its regional markets would add nearly $50 million to its bottom line. (Those regional markets do not include Las Vegas or Atlantic City, so this is just a fraction of the total possible opportunity.)

So here's what happened. Caesars' research, analytics, intuitions, and experience were distilled into the following five key Brown Shorts characteristics: initiate, know, delight, deliver, and own. Then Word Pictures descriptions were created for each characteristic. I can't share all of them with you—after all, what happens in Vegas, stays in Vegas—but I can show you some examples.

As a side note here, I need to mention that Word Pictures, like Brown Shorts, are meant to be customized to fit your culture. That's a good bit of what we do at Leadership IQ. So at Caesars, Needs Work and Great Work are now called Never Acceptable and Role Model—different words, same system.

Table 6-3 illustrates a few Word Picture examples from Caesars' "know" and "own" categories.

Now, having Word Pictures is great, but we do have to actually use them. So it was determined that these lessons in high performance would be taught via monthly learning activities. Each month, Caesars supervisors were trained in a short buzz session—five minutes dedicated to building an awareness of the Word Pictures that reflected that month's chosen topic (for example, "know" or "own").

Supervisors were then sent out into the field and directed to find appropriate real-life learning opportunities that addressed that month's topic and to deliver an individual 12-minute coaching session to each employee using those Word Pictures. Terry didn't sit employees in a class and pound initiate, know, delight, deliver, and own into their heads for eight hours. No, Caesars took its Word Pictures out of the classroom and onto the floor and used them as live coaching tools.

Table 6-3 Word Pictures from Caesars' "know" and "own"
categories

Never Acceptable. Guess or give out information of doubtful accuracy. Send the customer away without ensuring a suitable answer.	*Role Models*. When you don't know, thank your guests for their patience and maintain ownership until someone can help.
Never Acceptable. Fail to report new or difficult questions.	*Role Models*. Report new or difficult questions to your supervisor so he or she can investigate and get back to you.
Never Acceptable. Start your shift unprepared to answer the most common and important guest questions.	*Role Models*. Make it easy for your guests to get the answer by knowing the hours, prices, times, and locations of key property features and events.
Never Acceptable. Complain or speak negatively without offering legitimate suggestions for improvement.	*Role Models*. Be optimistic and speak positively about guests, coworkers, management, and the company. Offer helpful suggestions.

This works only because of Word Pictures' behavioral specificity and positive/negative example learning design. Abstract teaching or using only positive examples, as in most traditional workplace training programs, just doesn't work for this type of on-the-floor training.

Another bonus made possible by the design of Word Pictures was an employee self-evaluation. You see, this isn't just about managers teaching employees; it's about employees actually learning. So every month, coupled with the one-on-one coaching sessions, employees use Word Pictures to assess their own performance. This develops employees' critical self-awareness, and because of the behavioral specificity and learning design of Word Pictures, they immediately see where they should focus their personal improvement efforts.

Now, this is Caesars, so there are some sophisticated incentives tied to employee improvement. There's a tracking system for accountability, chips are awarded to reinforce behaviors, and more. But fundamentally, Terry will tell you this whole program is about changing what, where, and how employees learn about delivering excellent service.

Terry's not just a remarkably innovative service expert; he's also one heck of a training innovator. This cultural change does not require trainers, space, or formal scheduling. Simply put, there are no additional labor costs. And in a truly radical paradigm shift, employee development will eventually be owned by operations, not HR.

For an investment of 22 minutes per employee per month for six months, Caesars will get:

The most-willing-to-serve team members found anywhere.
Compelling answers to customer questions from the first
    employee asked.
The skill and attitude of employees becoming the most
    compelling reason to visit.

Maximized fulfillment, quality, and efficiency through
individual performance.

Extremely well-served guests because team members love
their work.

As I mentioned, Caesars has sophisticated proprietary models
that show exactly how much more customers spend when they're
delighted. Remember, even an extra $5 spent per customer at the
regional properties (not including Las Vegas or Atlantic City)
would add nearly $50 million to Caesars' bottom line. Since we're
"in" Las Vegas, let me put all my cards on the table: I'm not
allowed to divulge what the total payoff will be. But I can say that
a few Brown Shorts and Word Pictures, along with an innovative
training approach, are going to earn Caesars way more cash than
the typical marketing campaign or cost-cutting effort. And that's
no gamble. (Ba-dum-dum.)

Teaching with Word Pictures

Word Pictures can be used to onboard new employees, improve
existing employees, evaluate performance, give instructions, deliver
constructive feedback, and more. Many of the organizations we
work with apply Word Pictures as the foundation of their performance appraisals, and it's how they reward high performers.

Once you've got your Word Pictures defined, you're most of
the way there. Now all you've got to do is translate your work to
the organization at large. You don't want a Word Picture to be a
little slogan on the back of your name badge or a nice poster that
hangs on the wall. There are already enough fuzzy language mission statements hanging on boardroom walls.

For Word Pictures to successfully tackle bad attitudes and teach desired attitudes, they have to be reinforced everywhere, by every leader, every day in the organization. Here are some of the simplest and easiest techniques for transmitting a good attitude throughout the organization.

Co-opt Great Attitudes

One of the easiest techniques for teaching good attitude is to co-opt the high performing employees who already evidence your Great Work attitudes and behaviors. This involves an informal brainstorming session that will also help you flesh out the three categories of your Word Pictures.

Once you have a pretty good sense of the attitudes that drive organizational success, ask your high performers a couple of simple questions: What are the behaviors that you exhibit that make you successful in your job? What are the behaviors you see others exhibit that irritate you or cause you problems or limit their success?

A couple of things will happen. First, your high performers will have some great ideas about the specific behaviors that define Needs Work, Good Work, and Great Work. They'll make the job of completing your Word Pictures pretty darn easy for you.

The second thing that will happen is that high performers, when asked to help, will take even greater ownership of the Great Work behaviors outlined in your Word Pictures. It finally gives them some credibility to go talk to their peers and say, "Bob, your behavior when you were criticizing Joe during today's brainstorming session is in violation of what we said our standards were going to be here." By co-opting your high performers, you'll get them to do a lot of the teaching and enforcing of these behaviors for you. And that can be even more effective than when the boss does it.

Performance Management Systems

Too many performance appraisals are disconnected from the behaviors managers want to see. Look at how you're selecting, rewarding, praising, mentoring, and evaluating employees throughout the organization. Tie attitude to annual employee reviews and compensation by incorporating Word Pictures and behavioral language into your current process.

If a performance standard is not gradable, verifiable, and observable, it just isn't defined clearly enough. Take a look at your performance appraisals, and even if you can't alter your performance management tools, build some Word Pictures into the existing format. For example, if you have a place to offer comments on an annual review, add some of Word Pictures' descriptive language to your commentary. At least it will be a step in the right direction. And your employees will start to recognize that you've been paying extra special attention to the performance standard in question.

Conclusion

Leadership IQ has an entire consulting practice devoted to helping organizations develop Word Pictures. While we're aided by a big library of preexisting Word Pictures, it's important for our clients to remember that their Word Pictures need to reflect their unique cultures. It may seem as if it would be quicker to buy our library and call it a day, but that approach doesn't generate deep buy-in from employees—the people who will actually be living in the organization every day. So, by all means, use the examples in this chapter as a starting point and a teaching tool. But then work to make your Word Pictures reflect your organization's unique culture.

Conclusion

You now have the tools you need to inspire your employees to give their best efforts. The following 10 Hundred Percenter lessons reinforce the key insights shared in this book. Here you'll also find specific steps to help you get started using these tools to create a Hundred Percenter culture in your organization.

Hundred Percenter Lesson #1: Measure Your Culture

Well-designed employee surveys provide data that allows you to accurately assess your organizational culture. A great survey also helps identify where best to focus organizational time and resources toward building a Hundred Percenter culture. There is simply no faster way to communicate your Hundred Percenter desires than with great survey questions. However, most surveys are poorly designed.

If your current survey asks employees if they're "satisfied" but not if they're "inspired to give their best efforts," then you probably lack the data needed to build a Hundred Percenter culture. If your survey isn't asking questions that hit all the top engagement issues, and if every question doesn't have a clear path to action (i.e., you know what you need to do to address the issues being questioned), then once again, your survey is not serving you well.

Go back and review the Introduction and the kinds of questions Leadership IQ's Hundred Percenter Index asks. This will help you develop the techniques and questions you need to design a great employee survey. Once you've got your survey built, go ahead and survey your people. (As long as it's been at least six months since your last survey, you're in the clear.) Remember, every question you ask communicates your beliefs as a leader.

Hundred Percenter Lesson #2: Measure Your Leaders

Do you have 100% Leaders who create just the right levels of employee connection and challenge? Or do you have leaders who are Appeasers, Intimidators, or Avoiders? Creating a Hundred Percenter culture depends upon knowing exactly what kind of leaders drive the organization. Equally, leaders need to learn the truth about their current leadership style and acknowledge (and correct) any shortcomings it may include. This allows them to develop the critical self-awareness required to achieve significant change.

Once again, a good engagement survey can help. The Hundred Percenter Index builds queries about leadership styles and effectiveness right into the survey questions, and your survey should do the same. Once you've evaluated your leaders, you're ready for the next lesson.

Hundred Percenter Lesson #3: Make Every Goal HARD

The greatest successes result from HARD Goals, and that includes everyone's goals, not just your own. You can't ask (or expect) your employees to achieve greatness if their goals don't push them toward greatness. The same goes for trustees, vice presidents, managers, supervisors, and team leaders. Assess current goals to make sure they meet the HARD Goal criteria outlined in Chapter 1. If not, rewrite them so they do.

Hundred Percenter Lesson #4: Integrate HARD Goals and Word Pictures into Performance Management

If you set HARD Goals but then evaluate employees using an entirely different set of criteria, you won't get the desired results. Once HARD Goals are set, you still need to integrate those goals into every nook and cranny of your organization, including your performance management systems (e.g., performance appraisals). The Word Pictures technique you learned in Chapter 6 can be built right into your performance appraisals so you can be certain you are evaluating, rewarding, and coaching your people based on specific and clear performance expectations.

Hundred Percenter Lesson #5: Train Your Leaders to Be 100% Leaders

What's the first big step that an engineer takes on the road to becoming an engineer? Or a doctor? Or a lawyer? Or any other professional? The first step is training—hours and hours of training (high school, college, graduate school, professional education, etc.).

And yet the first steps to becoming a leader are typically promotion (for technical ability, not leadership skills), followed by getting an office, a budget binder, and a quick tutorial from HR on "how not to get sued." As a finish, we maybe give our leaders a pat on the back and a wish of "good luck" before pretty much abandoning them on the job.

Count the number of hours of formal, on-the-job training it takes to become a great professional. Then compare that with the number of hours of training you give your leaders. The huge discrepancy is why a lot of leaders fail to reach their full 100% Leader potential.

If you believe leadership is just common sense (and requires little to no skills or training), then you should be paying your leaders far less than your frontline employees. Why would anyone earn a six, seven, or eight figure salary for a job that's just common sense? However, if you believe it takes learned and practiced skills to become a 100% Leader (and that leaders are worth the money they get paid), then get started delivering leadership training right now. Visit www.leadershipiq.com for some suggested training outlines.

Hundred Percenter Lesson #6: Learn Everyone's Shoves and Tugs

Getting people motivated to become Hundred Percenters isn't that complicated; you just need to eliminate or neutralize employee Shoves (demotivators) and implement employee Tugs (motivators). But Shoves and Tugs conversations require leaders to be disciplined, courageous, and in possession of some interpersonal intelligence. That's why even though the techniques are elegantly simple, few leaders use them effectively without additional training.

Shoves and Tugs conversations may not go perfectly at first, but that's okay. Just get started and evaluate each conversation as it happens. Adjust your words and approach as needed to gain employee trust and to build deeper connection. Track your results. With persistence, the key drivers that motivate and demotivate your people should start to emerge in about 60 days. With each Shoves and Tugs conversation you have, it will become easier to identify the motivational levers that need to be pushed or pulled to create a culture of Hundred Percenters.

Hundred Percenter Lesson #7: Reach for Higher Stages of Accountability

What does a quick estimate of the Stages of Accountability (Denial, Blame, Excuses, Anxiety, and Accountability) in your organization tell you about how many of your employees live in each stage? (A good employee survey, like the Hundred Percenter Index, will tell you this with great accuracy.) I've yet to find an organization where every employee lives in perpetual accountability, but 100% Leaders come close. That's because they give feedback, lots and lots of feedback.

Just watch a professional sports team and pay attention to the feedback each player gets from the coach during the game. An NFL player might get 100 to 200 pieces of feedback (big and small) throughout a 60-minute game. By contrast, most employees maybe get 2 pieces of feedback a week, or even a month. And yet most leaders expect employees to deliver elite performance.

Elite athletes need lots of real-time feedback to be great, and so do Hundred Percenter employees. The IDEALS script lets you keep tough conversations free from emotional distraction so employees really hear your words and make needed behavioral changes to move into the Stage of Accountability.

Hundred Percenter Lesson #8: Turn Your Hundred Percenters into Heroes

At least once a week, tell a quick story of a Hundred Percenter (or of a Hundred Percenter effort given by an employee who's really trying). Your story should positively reinforce the individual and teach other employees how they can be Hundred Percenters too. CEOs might want to showcase the stories of a few frontline Hundred Percenters at the next board meeting (you can even ask those frontline folks to make an appearance and receive some thanks for their great work). Vice presidents can do the same at the next executive team meeting. Stop lamenting that there are no more great heroes and start putting your Hundred Percenters on display.

Hundred Percenter Lesson #9: Improve or Remove Talented Terrors

Repeat after me: "There's no such thing as a high performer with a bad attitude." Go out on the front lines and ask your Hundred Percenters how much they enjoy working with Talented Terrors. I've yet to see a situation where Hundred Percenters prefer working with Talented Terrors over working short staffed. One of the quickest ways to make a positive change to your organizational culture is to improve or remove your Talented Terrors. You'll feel like a weight has been lifted from your shoulders, and so will everyone else.

Hundred Percenter Lesson #10: Hire for Attitude

It's easier to build a Hundred Percenter culture when you hire folks with Hundred Percenter potential. Unfortunately, most hiring processes are so focused on skills that they neglect to assess whether or not candidates have a Hundred Percenter attitude.

Make your hiring process more effective by eliminating useless interview questions. Then find your Brown Shorts and turn them into Brown Shorts Interview Questions and Answer Guidelines. This will transform your hiring process and load your culture with Hundred Percenters.

Get Started Now

Don't stand on ceremony when creating a Hundred Percenter workplace. You don't have to wait until you get buy-in from every single person involved or until you have the budget to address every single piece. Get started now. Pick an area of critical importance (revamping goals, training leaders, surveying employees, etc.), and just get going. You don't need lots of fanfare. You just need for your leaders to read this book, to start discussing it, and then, bit by bit, to start challenging and connecting with employees.

Is it easier if the board and the CEO "get it" and commit every single leader and employee to the Hundred Percenter cause? Sure it is. But that level of buy-in takes time to achieve. Remember what the great anthropologist Margaret Mead said: "Never doubt that a small group of thoughtful, committed people can change the world. Indeed, it is the only thing that ever has."

Index

Leadership IQ Keeps Organizations and Their Leaders Nimble, Flexible, and Fast to Act

Leadership IQ is an elite boutique of experts serving virtually every industry with customized employee surveys, leadership training, and the tools for Hiring for Attitude.

Leadership IQ's Employee Engagement Surveys

For decades, employee engagement surveys have overlooked one critical element: *employees*. Think about it; we ask employees to take a survey, then their data goes off to some survey company, and the employees never see it again. Leadership IQ has revolutionized that process by discovering a whole new realm of engagement: *self-engagement*. For the first time ever, employees are active participants in driving their own engagement. After employees complete our engagement assessment, they get a detailed report that helps them diagnose and improve their personal levels of engagement. This is the most significant advance in the field since the actual creation of employee engagement surveys.

Leadership IQ's Leadership Training

We deliver leading-edge content with no fluff, and all of our training programs are customized and based on the latest research. Your managers get specific tools and scripts so they can take immediate action. Choose from our highly interactive on-site leadership training, our robust library of E-Learning Programs, online webinars, or bring Mark Murphy (the bestselling author of *Hundred Percenters*) on-site to deliver a custom keynote presentation.

Hiring for Attitude

Most organizations already know how to hire for skill. Now hiring managers can hire for attitude with the same confidence and accuracy. Whether you choose our customized Hiring for Attitude training program or our Hiring for Attitude certification program, your hiring managers will develop their "eye for talent" to recruit, interview, and make smart hiring decisions about the candidates who are the right attitudinal fit for your organization.

About the Author

Mark Murphy is the founder of Leadership IQ, an elite employee engagement and leadership training firm. His ongoing studies of more than 125,000 leaders across virtually every industry in North America, Europe, Asia, South America, and Australia are some of the largest in the world.

Mark's groundbreaking research studies make him a go-to source for major business press including *The New York Times*, the *Wall Street Journal*, *Fortune*, *Forbes*, *Bloomberg Businessweek*, *U.S. News & World Report*, and the *Washington Post*. His paradigm-shifting studies include "Job Performance Not a Predictor of Employee Engagement," "Are SMART Goals Dumb?" "Why CEOs Get Fired," "Why New Hires Fail," and "Don't Expect Layoff Survivors to Be Grateful."

A sought-after speaker, Mark has spoken at the United Nations, Harvard Business School, and Yale University, and he's been a featured guest on CBS News *Sunday Morning*, ABC's *20/20*, Fox Business News, NPR, and more.

Mark's work has helped thousands of organizations reach greater success including Aflac, Charles Schwab, Microsoft, IBM, MasterCard, Merck, MD Anderson Cancer Center, FirstEnergy, Ocean Spray, Volkswagen, Johns Hopkins, and more.

Mark's bestselling books are backed by rigorous research and offer leaders clear and actionable solutions. *Hiring for Attitude* was featured in *Fast Company* and the *Wall Street Journal* and was chosen as a top business book by *CNBC*. Some of his other titles include the international hardcover bestseller *Hundred Percenters: Challenge Your People to Give It Their All and They'll Give You Even More* and *HARD Goals: The Science of Getting from Where You Are to Where You Want to Be*.

Mark was awarded the prestigious Healthcare Financial Management Association's Helen Yerger Award for Best Research for being the first person to discover the link between layoff strategies and patient mortality rates. For his work in saving financially distressed hospitals, he was a three-time nominee for Modern Healthcare's Most Powerful People in Healthcare Award, joining a list of 300 luminaries including Hillary Clinton and George W. Bush. He is among only 15 consultants ever to be nominated to this list.

How Engaged Are You?

Throughout this book we discussed how to engage your employees. But have you ever wondered how your personal engagement stacks up?

Leadership IQ offers a free Self-Engagement Assessment to measure your own personal employee engagement. After you take the assessment, you'll immediately receive an 18-page report, your personal scorecard on 36 key self-engagement characteristics including:

- Are your goals exciting enough to help you get ahead at work?
- Have you given up control of your career to your boss (and how do you get it back)?
- Are you recovering quickly enough from emotional setbacks at work?
- Does your day "get away from you" as soon as you walk in the door?
- Are you currently setting yourself up to suffer from burnout?

Discover your personal engagement level at www.leadershipiq.com. And when you're ready to conduct this assessment for your whole organization, complete with customized reporting and benchmarking, just contact us at info@leadershipiq.com.

Become a Better Leader Online

D id you know that Leadership IQ is one of the world's largest providers of online leadership webinars? Be sure to check our full calendar of programs, such as:

- Hiring for Attitude
- Are You a Manager or a Leader?
- Overcoming a Culture of Entitlement
- The Secrets of Killer Presentations
- Speak the Truth Without Making People Angry
- Taking the Pain out of Performance Reviews

View our full calendar of webinars at www.leadershipiq.com.